Along the Way

The Life, Lessons, and Legacy of
Father Hugh F. Crean

FATHER MARK S. STELZER

Dedication

The College of Our Lady of the Elms
Chicopee, Massachusetts
Dedicates this Work
To the Memory of
Father Hugh Francis Crean, PhD, STD
(1937–2015)
Parish Priest, Professor and College Trustee, Visionary, and Friend
And to the Members of
The Crean and Andrews Families

In the face of a true friend, one finds a second self.
—Cicero, *De Amititia*

Contents

PART ONE

PART TWO

Foreword

I AM PARTICULARLY humbled by the invitation to write the foreword to this book honoring Father Hugh Crean, in whose honor the College of Our Lady of the Elms established the Father Hugh Crean Endowed Distinguished Lecture Series in 2019.

In so many ways, this book reflects the commitment of Elms College and our Saint Augustine Center for Ethics, Religion, and Culture to work collaboratively with the Diocese of Springfield in advancing our Catholic mission and the legacy of women and men like Father Hugh Crean, whose ministry has impacted the lives of so many people.

This book honors Father Crean's very special relationship with Elms College. A gifted classroom teacher, informed trustee, and honorary degree recipient, Father Crean was deeply committed to the vision of the Sisters of St. Joseph of Springfield who, in 1928, founded the College. At the same time, he was instrumental in helping Elms College realign its mission and programming in response to the changing needs of the Church and society. His keen financial sense helped guide Elms College through some very lean years.

I express sincere thanks to Father Crean's family for entrusting Elms College with the actual manuscripts and typescripts of material Father Crean hoped to publish. Because of their trust, the book their uncle, great-uncle, and brother-in-law envisioned has become a reality.

I am also most grateful to alumnae and other friends of Elms College who worked behind the scenes to get these manuscripts ready for publication. In particular, I thank Dr. Rosalie Ford ('62), who worked tirelessly with Father Crean in the late 1980s and 1990s to organize many of the homilies and other material found in this book. Without Dr. Ford's hard work and attention to detail, this book would not be. I also thank Sister Eileen Murphy ('69) and Mary Ellen O'Connor ('74) for dutifully reviewing the material organized first by Dr. Ford and later by Sister Margaret McCleary and Cheryl Willis. Finally, I thank Sister Angela Deady ('69) and Kathleen Gilhooly ('74) for editing the essays submitted by our contributors.

This book is of particular value insofar as it affords the reader (or listener) firsthand access to original material first written by Father Crean. Added value is found in the contributions of faculty members and friends of Elms College who expand on the major themes and foundations of Father Crean's work.

Sister Jane Morrissey, former member of the Elms College faculty and Father Crean's childhood friend, shares memories of Father Hugh's family and the formative influence of Saint Mary's Parish, and Saint Mary's Grammar and High School, all in Westfield, Massachusetts.

Dr. David O'Brien, former professor of history at Father Crean's alma mater, the College of the Holy Cross, shares a talk he first delivered at Elms College in 2021 in conjunction with the Reverend Hugh Crean Distinguished Lecture Series. In that talk, which has been adapted for this book, Dr. O'Brien considers some of the challenges society faced in the wake of Vatican II, which began in 1962, the same year Father Hugh was ordained.

Dr. Michael McGravey, assistant professor of religious studies and director of the Institute for Theology and Pastoral Studies at Elms College, explores Vatican II's invitation to shared ministry. Dr. McGravey also discusses some of the tensions and challenges of shared ministry that Father Hugh first highlighted in a talk delivered in 1984.

Sister Mary Johnson, congregational leader of the Sisters of Notre Dame de Namur and native of Sacred Heart Parish in Springfield, Massachusetts, where Father Crean ministered for many years, shares rich sociological and pastoral insight into what life and ministry in that inner-city parish looked and felt like in the last half of the twentieth century. Sister Mary also introduces us to Father Crean's cherished colleagues in ministry during his years at Sacred Heart. Sister Mary's essay is particularly pertinent, given that she was the inaugural speaker for the Reverend Hugh Crean Distinguished Lecture Series.

Dr. Peter DePergola, Shaughness Family Chair for the Study of the Humanities, executive director of the Saint Augustine Center for Ethics, Religion, and Culture, and associate professor of bioethics and medical humanities at Elms College, suggests ways in which theologian Paul Tillich, the subject of Father Crean's doctoral dissertation, impacted Father Crean's lifelong quest to understand the interplay of faith and doubt in the life of the believer. As chief ethics officer for Baystate Health, based in Springfield, Massachusetts, Dr. DePergola also describes how Crean's insights can be brought to bear in the care of patients and families living with complex medical diagnoses as they experience intermittent moments of great faith and great doubt.

Last but certainly not least, Father Mark Stelzer, special assistant to the president for Catholic identity, college chaplain, and associate professor of humanities at Elms College, invites us to consider ways in which Father Crean's priesthood of fifty-three years became, in effect, a "sacrament of friendship" for all who knew and loved him. It is no hyperbole to say that this project would not have taken place without the quiet leadership of Father Stelzer. He has been behind every aspect of it, from the initial contact with the family of Father Crean to the selection of the project contributors to the interaction with the publishing house. I express special thanks to Father Stelzer for the time and effort he has devoted as editor and leader of this project.

Father Crean's great mentor, Paul Tillich, reminds us that "the first duty of love is to listen." I invite you to listen with me to the voice of God that speaks to us through the pages of this book. At the same time, I invite you to listen with me to the voice of Father Hugh Crean encouraging us on our common journey "along the way."

Harry Dumay, PhD, MBA
President
College of Our Lady of the Elms
Chicopee, Massachusetts

Introduction

THIS COLLECTION OF homilies, reflections, and essays extends to those who knew Father Hugh Francis Crean (1937–2015) an invitation to listen once again to a familiar voice. At the same time, this collection affords an opportunity for those who never knew Hugh to listen for the first time to a voice that uplifted God's people in the Diocese of Springfield, Massachusetts, and beyond for more than fifty-three years.

Prior to his retirement from full-time ministry in 2005, Hugh spoke frequently of a desire to publish his homilies and talks. That hope only intensified during his retirement years. A handwritten prayer found among his papers reflects this hope:

> Lord, please give me one last energy to complete my work of
> writing and finishing my little project for humble publication.
> I am tired but I hope not yet finished.
> Help me, O God.

As a result of a diagnosis of Alzheimer's disease in 2005, Hugh was never able to publish. The contributors to this project are most grateful that Hugh did write an introduction, foreword, and outline for the work he envisioned. To no small extent, these pieces have guided the selection of material included in this book. These pieces were also helpful in the choice of authors invited to expand on the rich theological, ministerial, and pastoral insights found in Hugh's writings.

Hugh studied for the priesthood, undertook doctoral studies, and exercised priestly ministry during an exciting and pivotal period in Church history. Ordained a priest in 1962, just a few months prior to the start of the Second Vatican Council (1962–1965), Hugh was quick to realize the importance of implementing the reforms proposed by the Council. More importantly, Hugh recognized the importance of appropriating and living the spirit of the Council.

Diocesan leadership quickly recognized Hugh's keen intellect and pastoral sensibility. In 1969, he was assigned to doctoral studies at the University of Louvain in Belgium. At Louvain, Hugh chose to write his dissertation on the

German American Lutheran theologian Paul Tillich (1886–1965). Tillich's exploration of doubt as a structural element of faith intrigued Hugh and became the topic of his doctoral dissertation.

In addition to completing doctoral coursework and writing a dissertation while at Louvain, Hugh also served as spiritual director to students preparing for the priesthood. The years spent in this important ministry deepened Hugh's lifelong avocation to accompany priests in the joys and struggles of life and ministry.

Returning home from Louvain in 1973, Hugh found himself absorbed in the work of many diocesan committees and commissions established in the wake of Vatican II. He was an elected member of the first Priests Senate and the Bishop's Commission for the Clergy. In addition to his diocesan work, Hugh served on the faculty of the College of Our Lady of the Elms in Chicopee, Massachusetts. Hugh was a much-beloved professor of theology at what then was a small liberal arts college for women. At Elms College, his deep respect for the role of women in the Church and the Sisters of St. Joseph who taught him as a boy grew. It was during his Elms years that Hugh devoted much of his energy and writing to an exploration of Vatican II's invitation to shared and collaborative ministry. When the demands of his diocesan ministries increased and as requests to lead priest retreats multiplied, Hugh left the Elms in 1980.

Hugh's subsequent diocesan appointments as Director of Continuing Education for Priests, Consultor, and Vicar for Clergy only intensified his commitment to accompany his brother priests.

It should be noted that throughout his years of active ministry, Hugh always lived in a parish rectory. He shunned the "ivory tower" sought by many academics. Although technically assigned for many years to Sacred Heart Parish in Springfield, Massachusetts, as "priest in residence," Hugh nonetheless assisted with Mass coverage, baptized children, heard confessions, officiated at marriages, anointed the sick, counseled parishioners, and buried the dead. Hugh eventually ministered as co-pastor of Sacred Heart Parish with his lifelong friend Father George Farland. Hugh later served as pastor of two other vibrant parishes. Throughout his fifty-three years of priesthood, Hugh was the consummate parish priest.

Hugh retired from full-time ministry in 2004. In retirement, he lived at Providence Place in Holyoke, Massachusetts. There, Hugh was chaplain to the Sisters of Providence and other members of the retirement community. Hugh died in 2015. He was seventy-eight years old.

In February 2021, the administration of Elms College endorsed a proposal presented by faculty members to edit and prepare Hugh's work for publication. The project was placed under the auspices of the College's Saint Augustine Center for Ethics, Religion, and Culture, which sponsors the Reverend Hugh F. Crean Distinguished Lecture Series.

The family and friends of Hugh are honored by the willingness of Andrews McMeel Universal to publish this book. Jim Andrews, cofounder of the publishing house, was a childhood friend of Hugh. All of us associated with this project thank Jim's son, Hugh Andrews, chairman of Andrews McMeel Universal, for his enthusiastic support of this project. A special debt of gratitude is owed to our editor, Jean Lucas, whose guidance has been invaluable.

A work such as this brings together a diverse group of contributors. In the process of writing, contributors grow closer to one other. New friendships are formed, and old friendships are strengthened. I thank our contributors for their dedication to this project.

In the name of our contributors, I invite you to enjoy time spent with this book. I invite you to join us in thanking God for the life and ministry of Father Hugh Francis Crean.

Together, let's pray that Hugh now knows the joys of God's kingdom where, in the words Hugh often prayed as he concluded a funeral homily, "all lost things are found, all broken things are mended, all things forgotten are remembered, and all that we ever hoped for is ours for all eternity."

Father Mark S. Stelzer, STD
Special Assistant to the President for Catholic Identity
College of Our Lady of the Elms
Chicopee, Massachusetts
January 2022

Part One

Original Foreword

Hugh drafted this foreword in 1999 for use in a book of assorted homilies and talks he intended to publish in retirement.

I WOULD LIKE to express my gratitude to some very special people who have touched my life in wonderful and diverse ways.

First and foremost, I thank my deceased parents, Hugh and Nora Crean. Along with my deceased brothers, John and William, they were my first teachers. I also thank my sisters-in-law, Joan and Pat. Along with my 12 nieces and nephews, Joan and Pat bring great joy to my life.

I thank my sister, Sheila, and my close friend Sister Joan Ryzewicz. They have been my constant support and cherished companions in life.

I am also grateful to the priests and people of the Diocese of Springfield with whom I have shared ministry.

I had a boyhood friend. His name was James Andrews. We grew up in the city of Westfield, Massachusetts, and enjoyed each other's company and friendship as we were sneaking up on the mystery of adulthood. Unfortunately, he died too young at the age of 44.

I became a priest and Jim found his home in publishing and creative art. Jim succeeded in business and in life. He found a wonderful wife, Kathleen Whalen Andrews. They were blessed with two sons, Hugh Timothy and James Frederick. Like their mother and father, Hugh and James are my lifelong friends.

I dedicate my modest production to Jim, Kathleen, and their sons. I also dedicate this work to my family.

Rosalie Ford has been an invaluable assistant to me in the selection and preparation of texts for publication. I thank Rosalie and Sister Eileen Murphy who graciously assisted with the typing of my manuscripts.

Finally, I am grateful to so many people who taught me to be a priest. I am grateful for all that I have learned from them "along the way."

First Mass—Father Francis Reilly

Hugh delivered this homily in Our Lady of Hope Church in Springfield, Massachusetts, in 1980. The homily honors Hugh's cousin, Father Francis Reilly. Hugh also delivered the homily at Father Reilly's 25th Anniversary Mass.

IT IS VERY easy to sense the pride and happiness of today's congregation as we celebrate together the first Mass of Francis Reilly. We welcome and congratulate his parents, Mitch and Peg Reilly, brother Steve and his wife Linda, Senator Marty, Meg and Gene, grandmother Hannah Shea, Father Tom Courtney, parishioners of Our Lady of Hope, relatives, and friends. This is a beautiful family and parish day for all of us.

In the Emmaus gospel just read for us, dusk is falling; the sun is setting; the heat of the day is past. Two men are walking along discussing their fears, disappointments, problems, and their world view. They are discouraged and afraid. Jesus comes into their midst and unfolds the Scriptures. He brings healing to their troubled hearts. He breaks bread with them, and their spirits burn with a new zeal and a new purpose. He helps them to see themselves and their world in a new way.

This is a most appropriate gospel for Fran's Mass today. It speaks of that invitation that is now his as a priest to walk through life with people, to live among them as a companion, and to be a preacher and healer.

For Francis the journey toward this day began a long time ago. The blood of the Reillys, Healys, Sheas, and Creans who hail from the rocky coast of Galway and Kerry have shaped and formed him. His experience of family and parish life here on Hungry Hill, and all he learned at Norwich and Louvain, called Francis to walk a road less traveled in the priesthood of Jesus Christ.

Francis has received the great and precious gift of recognizing and responding to the call of Jesus and the Church. Gathered with him for his First Mass, we realize that this is a gift intended to be shared with others. Fran is a messenger of God's Word. Like Jesus who walks with the Emmaus disciples, Fran now walks the road of life with God's people, sharing their dreams, their joys, and their sorrows.

In the priesthood, Fran will rejoice with the happy, grieve with the sorrowing, talk deep into the night with the troubled and doubting. He will hear the pain of the confused, hope with the uncertain, love with the passionate, sing and laugh with the young, and pray with the lonely.

Today is a great day for our Church, our family, and the presbyterate of the Diocese of Springfield. We celebrate a new beginning for a man and friend whom we are proud to have as a priest among us.

Today, Jesus says to Fran, "Walk with me for I wish to use your heart to love, your lips to speak and pray, your hands to heal, and your eyes to see the needs and hopes of people. I invite you to dream, to celebrate the sacrament of healing love in Eucharist and the sacrament of friendship in priesthood."

Fran, know that you are not alone. You have our support and our love as you continue to be shaped and formed by people of God you will serve.

We rejoice with you Francis, our brother, our priest, and our friend.

We rejoice because the Lord has placed a marvelous love in your heart for us and all his people to share.

25th Anniversary of Ordination— Father Leo O'Neill

This homily was preached in Saint Mary's Church in Haydenville, Massachusetts, in 1980, in celebration of the 25th anniversary of Father Leo O'Neill's ordination to the priesthood. Just a few days prior to the celebration, Father Leo had been named Auxiliary Bishop of Springfield.

TODAY'S GOSPEL REMINDS us that Jesus' primary concern was always for the whole person. After spending an entire day teaching his disciples, Jesus wanted to make certain that they were fed.

As we read through the pages of the New Testament, we can't help but notice that Jesus was constantly responding to all sorts of human needs. When people were sick, he healed them; when they were lonely, he included them; when they were ignorant, he taught them; when they sinned, he forgave them; when their hearts were broken, he comforted them; and when they were hungry, he fed them.

We also notice when reading the New Testament that Jesus called his disciples to join him in ministering to the diverse needs of God's people. For 25 years, Leo has met the many needs of God's people. Leo has:

- Rejoiced with the happy;
- Grieved with the sorrowing;
- Talked deep into the night with the troubled and the doubting;
- Heard and shared the pain of the confused;
- Hoped with the uncertain;
- Loved with the passionate;
- Struggled with the little ones;
- Prayed with the lonely ones.

Above all, for 25 years Leo has invited people to gather for the Eucharist and to be fed with the bread that gives life today and promises new life tomorrow.

Father Leo was ordained to the priesthood 25 years ago by Bishop Weldon. However, he was consecrated in priesthood by the people of Saint Mary's Westfield, Saint Catherine's Springfield, Saint Mary's Haydenville, and by the hundreds of men and women, priests and religious sisters who are part of the fabric of his life. We have all shaped his priesthood. We have evoked the best of his gentle, yet strong personality.

Leo has been formed by his family and the Elmwood section of Holyoke. He has been formed by nuns and bells of Saint Mary's in Westfield, the parks and homes of the Sixteen Acres in Springfield, and the happy hills of Haydenville.

Today is a great day for our Church and for our Diocese. We celebrate 25 years of Leo's ministry as a priest and his new ministry as a bishop among us. To our friend and brother, priest and bishop, the Lord says, "Come and walk with me to the place I will show you."

Leo, the Lord loves you. His Church and we, His people, love you.

The Lord needs you to preach the just word and to celebrate over and over again the great sacrament of Eucharist. He needs you to strengthen the bond of fraternity among your brothers who share with you in the sacrament we call "priesthood."

The Lord wishes to use:

- Your heart to love;
- Your lips to speak and pray;
- Your hands to feed and heal;
- Your bishop's staff to shepherd;
- Your inner poet to craft words that challenge and offer hope.

Leo, as we look back with gratitude on your yesterdays, we also look towards your tomorrows and offer you, our brother, our friend, our priest, and now, our bishop, heartfelt thanks. You have shared your life with us and have sealed our hearts with the mark of Christ's priesthood.

Today we celebrate much more than the day of your priesthood ordination. We celebrate your entire life: a life of attending to the needs of so many people in so many ways. As you undertake your ministry as a bishop in our midst, know of our admiration, support, and great love.

Liturgy of Christian Burial— Sister Thomasine O'Connor, SNDdeN

Sister Thomasine O'Connor served as pastoral minister at Sacred Heart Parish in Springfield, Massachusetts, during Hugh's tenure as a priest in residence and co-pastor. A native of Sacred Heart Parish, Sister Thomasine was influential in forming the parish's Over Sixty Club. This homily was delivered in 1986.

IN A BEAUTIFUL book entitled *Ireland: A Terrible Beauty,* there is a picture of a man from the wild, rugged coast of West Kerry. The man stands proud and strong with bright eyes and a beguiling smile. The caption beneath the picture reads, "Have yourself a good look now, for when I'm gone you'll never see the likes of a man like me, again."

How appropriate is this sentiment as we honor the life and person of Sister Thomasine O'Connor, our dear friend, co-worker, and Sister of Notre Dame.

Thomasine's veins flowed with the blood and vitality of her Kerry parents. She was born Katherine Frances O'Connor and was baptized here at Sacred Heart Church in 1918. She grew up in this neighborhood, attended Sacred Heart Elementary and High School, and entered the Sisters of Notre Dame in 1939. From there began her journey of ministry and service to countless people privileged to call her Sister and friend.

After her profession, Sister Thomasine spent 21 years at Emmanuel College as a cook. Then, in a spirit of mission and adventure, she went to Japan. She spoke with fondness and affection about her formative and missionary years in Japan. Next came her phenomenally productive years here in her home parish, first as a kindergarten teacher and then as a vital part of our pastoral team.

What can we say of Sister Thomasine?

I compare her life and ministry to that of Christ Himself.

Like Jesus, who spent 30 years in the background listening, observing, and reflecting in silence, Thomasine lived a quiet life in the kitchen at Emmanuel College in Boston. Like Jesus, who eventually burst into the spotlight during his years of public ministry, Thomasine burst into the spotlight in parish ministry, doing the very same things Jesus did during his years of public ministry. In imitation of Jesus, Thomasine taught and healed. She gave comfort to the sick and grieved with the mourning. She laughed and cried with the rich and the poor. In recent months, she bore the Cross which a cancer diagnosis brings.

Everyone here knows that, like Jesus, Thomasine was at home with all kinds of people. She could be seen in the downtown soup kitchen or in the homes of the rich. She brought God's peace to the elderly whenever she brought the Eucharist to their homes or apartments. Thomasine brought laughter to Over 60 Club meetings, trips, and parties. She organized a food fund for the poor and Thanksgiving dinners for the needy. She brought flowers to nursing homes.

At Sacred Heart, Thomasine taught kindergarten and supervised religious education classes. She was especially proud of each year's First Communion class. She loved Baptism preparation classes and conducted them with a special grace. Nervous brides met her for wedding rehearsals and usually left with a smile on their faces and appreciation in their hearts. Thomasine sold raffle tickets anywhere and everywhere for the benefit of the parish or some worthy organization like the Hibernians. She had an energy and purpose that was boundless. She was playful and completely without guile or pretense.

Who could ever forget the antics and unpredictability of Sister Thomasine? She dressed as Santa Claus at Christmas and was a vision in green on Saint Patrick's Day. She wore crazy hats and costumes. She flew through the streets (and sometimes through stop signs!) in her car. She struck fear into the hearts of travel agents if they did not meet the high standards she set for her Over 60 Club trips.

Thomasine could not always tell you exact names and addresses. Such things simply were not important. Although she might confuse a Foley with an O'Brien, a Mary with a Catherine, a Catjakis with a Dukakis, Thomasine knew hearts and homes. She knew the needs behind the doors of so many whose lives she touched.

Who will ever forget some of her favorite expressions? After each trip she would say with great enthusiasm, "This was the best ever!" When things went right, she said, "Everything is in perfect order." When someone died, she would remark, "She has gone to God." We remember her many comical renditions of "Please Release Me, Let Me Go," and her quip after each successful endeavor: "Now I'm ready for a liquor ball."

Thomasine always and everywhere wanted to make George and me look good. She taught us much about what it means to be a team. We respected her, laughed with her, cried with her, and loved her.

There were many sides to our Sister Thomasine. She could sing and dance with the best. Her Irish spirit was happy, fun-loving, and optimistic. Yet, as her niece so beautifully put it, that carefree spirit was balanced by a firm commitment to the vowed life she lived as a Sister of Notre Dame. This commitment was as real to Thomasine as life itself. She lived her vocation with grace. She lived a balanced and good life.

These last few months were not easy ones for Thomasine. In imitation of Jesus, she endured a mystical crucifixion. This was her last and most noble ministry to all of us as a woman and a Sister of Notre Dame.

It's appropriate that Sister Thomasine died in the season of All Saints. Saints come in all sizes and shapes, nationalities, and personalities. It is not the size of the halo or piety that makes a saint. It is quality of life and goodness that make a saint. We praise and thank God for the quality and goodness of Thomasine's life.

"Have yourself a good look now, for when I'm gone you'll never see the likes of a man like me again." Although in many ways we will never see the likes of Thomasine again, her piercing blue eyes, irrepressible spirit, and quick movement in step will live on in us. We will see the likes of Thomasine every time we imitate her life of service and joy.

Sister Thomasine, with Julie your foundress, may you rest peacefully in the love of a God who truly is so good!

National Honor Society Induction

Hugh delivered this address in 1987 at Cathedral High School in Springfield, Massachusetts, where three of his own high school teachers served. At the time of this address, Sister Patricia James was principal of Cathedral High School. Sister Marita Joseph and Sister Theresa Derouin served as faculty members.

I AM HONORED to be here this evening at the invitation of the graduating class and school administrators to celebrate this very special occasion with you.

I am particularly delighted to be reunited with Sisters Marita Joseph, Theresa Derouin, and Patricia James. They were my teachers at Saint Mary's High School in Westfield. Today, they are your teachers.

Saint Mary's was a small, but proud and good school. I stand here today forever grateful to the Sisters of St. Joseph for their dedication to the work of Christian education: a work they continue to carry out today at Cathedral High School and in so many other ministries.

I come here this evening as one of another generation to bask in your idealism, share your faith, encourage your scholarship and service, celebrate the honors you have earned, and to be ignited by your fire.

One would think that your invited speaker—already beyond midlife—would attempt to share practical lessons or give advice based on his own experience: "This is what I have learned" or "This is what you should do." I intend to do neither.

What I intend to ask of you tonight is nothing new. Although not new, what I ask of you is mine. What I ask of you is shaped and formed by my own convictions.

Tonight, I ask you to become dreamers. In a world of knowledgeable cynics, skilled technicians, and practical realists, I certainly encourage you to be knowledgeable and competent. Yes, you need the skills required to earn a just and living wage. However, as you learn those skills, hold on to the dreams and visions of your youth. Allow your youth-filled dreams and visions to shape your tomorrow and today.

Your years at Cathedral High School have prepared you for life. You have studied mathematics and science. You have been enriched by the humanities.

Some of you have taken courses designed to help you excel in the world of business.

Above and beyond the many names and dates you have memorized, the theories you have explored, and the business practices you have mastered, your years at Cathedral High School have fostered in each of you an appreciation of the One, the True, the Beautiful, and the Good. Taken together, these four so-called "transcendentals" are the very source from which dreams emerge and by which dreams are sustained.

In so many ways, our individual and collective dreams this day flow from the firm belief that in Jesus, the ultimate dreamer, each of us is called and has something important to say and do for our world and Church.

The Gospel of John has much to say about Jesus' dream for his followers of all ages, including you the graduates of 1988. In what is commonly referred to as his "Priestly Prayer," Jesus asks three things of his disciples. He asks that they be one. He asks that they be accountable. He asks that they be sent.

Tonight, we pray that you, our graduates, will be one with all you encounter in the years to follow despite any differences in race, nationality, or religion. We ask that you be one despite ideological or political differences. We ask that you live life with a spirit of reverence for others.

Tonight, we pray that you will be accountable and good stewards of the many gifts God has given you. We ask that you care a little more and love a little more because of your Cathedral education and all you have learned of Christ.

Tonight, as you are sent forth from this school, we pray that you will have something of meaning to say to the world that desperately awaits your witness and all the good you will say and do.

This is a night of celebration.

We congratulate you and your parents on the honors you receive.

We ask you to be successful, ambitious, efficient, and productive.

Teilhard de Chardin once said, "Someday, after mastering the winds and waves, the tides and gravity, we shall harness for God the energies of love, and then, for a second time in the history of the world, man will have discovered fire."

Is it possible that this can be our collective dream: to harness for God the energies of love?

Is it possible that this can be your own dream?

I think so. And so do those who love you and honor you today.
May God bless you today.
And, may God bless all of your tomorrows yet to come.

150th Anniversary—Sisters of Notre Dame de Namur

This homily was delivered in conjunction with a televised Mass in 1990 marking the 150th anniversary of the arrival of the Sisters of Notre Dame in the United States. Sister Mary Johnson, a contributor to this volume, was interviewed following the Mass. A link to a recording of this televised Mass is found in the appendix to this book.

WHEN PEOPLE KNOW they have less than 24 hours to live, whatever they say or do is important.

If you had only 24 hours to live, what would you say or do?

Today, we look at what Christ said and did on the day before he died. He took His closest friends, went to a special place, and celebrated the Last Supper. He spoke words and performed an act of timeless meaning. At that table, Jesus took bread, and He took the cup. He then said, "This is My body. This is My blood. Do this in remembrance of Me."

Ever since that day, the Eucharist has been celebrated in catacombs, in stately cathedrals, in monasteries, in ordinary parish churches, in hidden rooms in persecuted countries. Wherever in what circumstances it has been celebrated, the Eucharist has always been a sign of the sustaining, loving presence of the Lord.

The night before He died, Jesus not only celebrated the Eucharist. He also uttered important words as His last will and legacy of remembrance.

Our gospel reading for today is part of that farewell address spoken by Jesus before his death. With deep love and care for His disciples and those who would come after them, He said, "I will never leave you alone. I will send you the Holy Spirit to be with you always."

The promised Spirit would come and, like Jesus, teach, lead, comfort, and strengthen. The Spirit would be a friend and guide. What a consoling and gracious gift those first disciples and we have in the Spirit.

In a special way today, we celebrate a particular manifestation of the saving work of the Spirit who continues to inspire the Church in every age.

Come back with me 150 years to October 19, 1840, when eight Sisters of Notre Dame de Namur, a religious community founded by Saint Julie Billiart, arrived in the United States from Belgium. The Sisters settled in Ohio and ministered to the many needs of the immigrant Church there. In 1867, a small group came to Holy Name, Chicopee; in 1869, to Saint Jerome's, Holyoke; and in 1877, to Sacred Heart, Springfield. They established the first Catholic schools in our Diocese in Chicopee, Holyoke, and Springfield. They planted the seeds of faith in the hearts and minds of thousands of young people in western Massachusetts.

The promise of Christ to send the Spirit was embodied generously and lovingly in the zeal, courage, and devotion of those first Sisters of Notre Dame. From the beginning, their work and mission embraced the poor and needy, especially the poor children in schools they founded throughout our country and abroad.

In the Diocese of Springfield, hundreds of Sisters of Notre Dame have endeared themselves to grateful students and families for 120 years. Having lived at Sacred Heart for the past 17 years and having served with the Sisters of Notre Dame, I can personally speak of the great respect, love, and affection of the priests and people for these, our Sisters.

In recent years, the Sisters have embraced many other ministries besides teaching. Here, at Sacred Heart, they were instrumental in founding the Spanish Apostolate. Today, they are engaged in parish ministry and serve in health care settings.

Although the Sisters of Notre Dame ask nothing of us, we owe them an immense debt of gratitude as we rejoice with them in this 150th anniversary year.

Sisters, your work is not finished. The promise of the Spirit to teach, guide, comfort, and strengthen is enfleshed in your witness. With you, we cherish your proud past. We celebrate your creative ministerial dedication today. We join with you in hope and optimism as you meet the many opportunities and challenges of tomorrow.

In that timeless moment long ago, when Jesus sat down at table with His disciples, He said that the Father would send us the Spirit to be with us always. He promised that his disciples of all ages would do even greater things than He. That promise sustains us and is embodied in the spirit-filled gifts of generous service which you, the Sisters of Notre Dame, consistently share with all God's people.

We pray today for and with all Sisters of Notre Dame who, in the spirit of Julie Billiart, remind us each day of the goodness of the good God.

Day of Recollection for Priests

The is the talk Hugh delivered to priests of the Diocese of Worcester in 1990. This is one of more than 100 retreat talks and conferences Hugh delivered over a period of 25 years in the United States and beyond.

A DAY OF recollection in Lent is not only a time for personal inventory of faults and examination of conscience. It is also a time to be strengthened, encouraged, and supported in the life and ministry we share as priests.

The last three chapters of Hebrews give us three reasons for encouragement. Those chapters speak to us of:

- The amazing graces we have all received;
- The sacrifices already made and the heroes who have gone before us;
- The faith that called us to ministry and the fidelity of Christ that sustains us.

I encourage you as we gather today to count some of the victories, to rejoice in the good works that you have done and are doing. I also invite you to affirm one another and those with whom you work.

As we look around the room on a day like this, we realize that we are a diverse lot. We vary in age and ideology. We vary in language and culture. Yet, we are one. In a special way, you are one: one presbyterate committed to the People of God living in the Diocese of Worcester.

I spend a lot of my time these days traveling throughout the United States and Canada offering days of recollection and retreats for priests. I have listened to priests just like yourselves. I have learned that despite their oneness, presbyterates often find themselves divided. I have also learned that this division is frequently rooted in generational differences between and among younger, middle-aged, and senior clergy. We often lack an appreciation of the unique challenges faced by priests, particularly priests of a different generation than our own. I would like to spend this first conference addressing that generational divide. I would like to speak a word to our senior priests, middle-aged priests, and younger priests.

What can we say to our senior priests?

Each of you has already invested so much of your life. You have been an amazing grace to so many people in your years of ministry. We ask you today to encourage us as we become involved in the issues of our day, just as you passionately cared for the causes of your youth and middle years. You still have a ministry to share. Like Simeon and Anna, you optimistically proclaim the beginning of a new day. Like Abraham and Zechariah, yours is a ministry of faith and hope. You share wisdom forged by experience. You know more than we do. You have learned so much we need to learn. You have been to places of the heart that we have not yet discovered.

We ask that you help us with your prayers. We invite your confidence in each of us. Share with us your experience. Tell us of your hopes. Although you have no children of your own, thousands have called you "Father" and hold your name and ministry in affectionate remembrance.

We ask that you forgive us when we get careless or when we forget your sacrifices and services of yesterday and today.

We ask that you show us the way to live. Help us to keep a sense of humor. Teach us the way to grow in age, wisdom, and grace. We need mentors and brothers like you to guide us along the way. Please know of our appreciation for you.

What can we say to our middle-aged priests?

The burden of administration and the pastorate is in your hands. Your task is great. The expectations of bishops, older and younger priests, and laypersons are high. They challenge you to be a leader, a visionary, a preacher, a teacher, a pastor, an office manager, a financier, and a mystic. Your lives get cluttered; your vision sometimes gets blurred; your goals become skewed. Do not be discouraged when you cannot do everything well. Know that you have collaborators in ministry who are also called to serve. We invite you to open the way for them. Share your ministry with them. Become a sign of hope and optimism to those who come after you. Know of our gratitude for your witness and service.

What can we say to our younger priests?

You have vitality, energy, cultural understanding, and zeal. Your experience of priesthood is still fresh and new. You will undertake countless programs. There are new ideas you will test and risks you will take. People you have yet to meet will form you as priests. You will be with countless people in moments of joy and sadness. You are our hope. The Church needs your commitment, optimism, courage, and leadership.

Be patient and trusting of us who are older than you are. Be tolerant of reluctance to change. Affirm and befriend us. We need one another. Please know of our appreciation for you and your priesthood.

Christmas

Hugh delivered this homily in 1991 while major renovations were being undertaken in Sacred Heart Church in Springfield, Massachusetts. This was Hugh's last Christmas at Sacred Heart Parish. He was reassigned in 1992 to Holy Name Parish, also in Springfield.

CHRISTMAS IS DIFFERENT at Sacred Heart this year. Our church, normally dressed in regal splendor with an abundance of flowers, subdued candlelight, and a beautiful manger scene, is choked with scaffolding. As we await completion of the renovations, the church seems unfinished and imperfect.

In so many ways, the unfinished and imperfect appearance of our church reminds of the message of Christmas. Like our church this year, the place of Christ's birth was not quite right. He was born in a stable and placed in a bed of straw. God's gift of his own self came, not in royal splendor, but in the weakness of a newborn child.

What was special about that first Christmas was not the place, but the people; not the decorations, but the attitude; not the glory, but the simplicity. The Christmas story is a very simple story of a caring father, Joseph, and a loving mother, Mary. It is a story of a stable and of no room in the inn.

Today we come very close to Joseph and Mary. We recognize their goodness and faith. We honor their simplicity. Mary and Joseph teach us and guide us. They teach us to value the things that really matter at Christmas and throughout the year.

Beyond all that is good and human in Mary and Joseph we find the divinity of Jesus, the Christ of God. Today, God unmasks himself and becomes a baby. Though helpless and dependent, the Babe of Bethlehem says to us, "I am with you."

To whom did the Child of Bethlehem come?

He came to those in need. He came to the confused and the hurting. This child came to the sick and the disabled, the poor and the troubled. He came to the rich and the restless, the doubter and the cynic.

To each he says, "I am with you. I can help you from my crib in Bethlehem, from my cross on Calvary, from my home in Heaven. This is why I came and why I live: to help you."

This is the eternal story of Christmas. This is a story not lost in abstractions of theology but dramatized in human history. This is a story that inspires hope in adults and brings excitement to children.

The most common gesture of Christmas is gift giving—a sign that we understand what God wants this feast and season to mean to the world. I suggest that each of us give away this Christmas Mass to someone we love and to a world of people who need love as our special celebration of the birth of Christ. Then together we can ask the Lord:

> O Child of Bethlehem, House of David, Man of Jerusalem,
> City of Peace,
> You have loved us without limit or condition.
> You have loved us in our greatness and in our misery, in our folly
> and in our virtue.
> Let Your hand of guidance be upon us, and may Your heart be
> within us so that we too may become bread and peace for
> one another.

In the name of Father Farland and in the name of our wonderful parish staff, I wish you all a Merry Christmas.

Celebration of Special Anniversaries—Sisters of St. Joseph

Hugh regularly celebrated Community Masses with the Sisters of St. Joseph of Springfield. This homily was delivered in 1992 at Mont Marie in Holyoke, Massachusetts.

THIS IS A beautiful day of rejoicing as we honor our jubilarians who celebrate 50 and 25 years of religious profession.

Our jubilarians have chosen "Gathered in Wisdom" as their jubilee theme. On a day like this, we realize that above all riches, possessions, achievements, and honors, wisdom is the jewel of greatest price. Women and men of substance have always known the value of wisdom. Religious life has consistently reinforced its value. The women we honor today have sought this great jewel called wisdom for the last 50 or 25 years.

What is this biblical jewel, this pearl of great price about which the Scriptures speak? It is neither silver nor gold; it is neither fame nor status. Wisdom is an attitude and a way of life. Wisdom is an inner yearning that says we are stronger when we seek the *maius*, that is, the ever greater. Wisdom means many things:

It means carefully observing the world around us, recognizing the things that really matter.
It means reflecting on the lilies of the field, the birds of the air, and learning timeless lessons from them.
It means observing old and young people who are signs of unselfishness and generosity for us to imitate.
It means not making judgements rashly.
It means giving and receiving forgiveness and offering people a second chance.
It means listening when we are tempted to speak.

It means finding the right words to speak at the right time, and for
the right reason.
It means balance, tolerance, optimism, and hope.

We pray for such wisdom today as we honor the community of the Sisters of St. Joseph who have fostered in its members and in all of us knowledge and values which are the roots of wisdom.

Today we honor 16 women who have embraced the life of a Sister of St. Joseph in generosity and faith. I stand before you representing thousands of people who would like to express their own gratitude for what you and your witness means to them. In their name, I thank you for your ministry, witness, and wisdom.

As we celebrate our golden jubilarians, we realize that their journey to today began in 1942 in the midst of World War II. In 1942, our nation was poised for a long war. As your high school classmates and family members were making a commitment to military service, you, as very young women, were also making a commitment: a commitment to the Church and God's people.

As we celebrate our silver jubilarians, we realize how different the world was when they entered religious life 25 years later. In 1967, our nation was again at war, this time in Vietnam. We were still grieving the end of the Kennedy era and hearing the promise of Lyndon Johnson's Great Society. We saw Flower Children on the streets of San Francisco and listened to the Beatles on transistor radios. We were part of war protests and saw riots erupt following the passage of civil rights legislation.

When our silver jubilarians entered religious life, Vatican II had ended. The world and the Church were changing fast. These jubilarians heard a call from God in unique times and responded to the mystery of a call to the vowed life. This meant leaving family and friends behind and becoming part of a religious congregation still discerning the changing signs of the times.

In 1942 and in 1967, a special faith was required to make the decision that you, our jubilarians, made. That decision led you to teach in Catholic schools from Pittsfield to Newport. That decision led you to daycare centers, parish ministry, campus ministry, homeless shelters, health care ministries, congregational leadership, and community service.

In early days, your decision to enter religious life entailed long days of regimented prayer. It meant teaching school all day and then engaging in

Confraternity of Christian Doctrine classes and other parish responsibilities with little time for self. That decision meant—and continues to mean—a sacrifice of security in a changing world and Church. It meant—and continues to mean—walking with Abraham to the place God will show.

Jubilarians, your journey is far from over! Your witness—strong and brave—remains a sign to us, your brothers and sisters, who admire and respect you. Your witness teaches all of us how to be faithful and how to be Church.

Your quest for wisdom continues. Each day brings new challenges and new questions as individually and collectively you seek and live that wisdom which teaches us that faith is greater than fear.

Today, the questions and decisions are different than they were in 1942 and 1967. We rejoice in knowing that what remains the same is your commitment to be the wisdom seekers we love and honor today.

Through the intercession of Saint Joseph, may God bless you this and every day!

Retreat Conference

Hugh gave this talk in 1992 on an extended retreat for priests in Ontario, Canada. Hugh adapted this particular talk many times for use in other dioceses and religious communities.

MY NAME IS Hugh Crean. I have been ordained 37 years and am a pastor in Massachusetts. I feel I represent the average parish priest ordained in the late '50s and early '60s. I attended the seminary while Vatican II was in progress and was profoundly influenced by its spirit and teaching. With the exception of the years I spent in Louvain for doctoral studies, I have spent my entire priesthood, even while involved in diocesan administration, engaged in parish ministry. All these things give me no special credentials, but I feel I already know you. I feel at home with you.

We move, often clad in black, among people every day as signs of contradiction. We point to the divine as we stand in the person of Christ and say words like "Do this—all of this—in memory of me." We attempt to share a vision which sometimes even we, ourselves, only glimpse "through a glass darkly." Like Jeremiah, we speak a word that is not our own. That word burns like a fire within us. That word takes on our weakness and invites us to serve. All this we do for the sake of God's people.

As priests, we live by our wits, an expression I use for the intellectual, educational, and technical skills we bring to our ministry.

As priests, we live by our words as we preach, counsel, and teach.

As priests, we live by a type of wisdom that informs and surpasses our wit and words. Our wisdom reflects the accumulation of life experience. It forges values and informs our decisions. Wisdom centers our lives.

What fuels our wits, words, and wisdom in the work we do? The traditional source of our spiritual energy is, and always will be, prayer. Thus, the subject of our talk: Practical Prayer for the Busy Priest.

So what do we mean by prayer, practical, and busy?

Prayer implies something essential to the Christian life and to our life as priests. We engage in prayer every day as we celebrate the Eucharist and pray the Breviary.

Practical implies something that is doable, realistic, fulfilling, and appropriate.

Busy implies living in the hectic setting of a rectory that is not always compatible with contemplation. Busy also suggests the pace of our daily life as priests.

If I were to choose the one verse in the New Testament that describes what we, as disciples, are called to be, I would choose Mark 3:15: "Be my companions; preach my word; heal my people."

Being a priest requires us to bring healing to countless people in countless ways. Each of us brings that healing in his own way. Sometimes we heal others by the words we speak. More often, that healing occurs in silence.

We preach the Gospel by what we say and do each day as we celebrate Eucharist. We preach the Gospel as we carry out various ministries. We preach the Gospel as we interact with countless individuals each day. Yet, at the very foundation of all healing and preaching are those words of Mark quoted above: "Be my companions; preach my word; heal my people."

How do we become companions of the Lord in the busy world in which we live?

Here, I suggest six movements or "postures" in prayer that can be undertaken as we strive to be Jesus' companions. The movements/postures in prayer are self-acceptance, self-surrender, contrition, acceptance of God's love, petition, and thanksgiving.

Taken individually, each of these six movements/postures keeps us in touch with God, with others, and with ourselves. Taken collectively, these six movements/postures represent a form of centering prayer.

Self-acceptance

I sit, drive, walk, and run with the Lord as my companion. In this first movement of prayer each day, I accept the fact that I am accepted just as I am today, not as the person I was yesterday nor as the person I will be or want to be tomorrow. I am accepted as I am with my many gifts and glaring faults.

Self-surrender

I give my accepted self to God in an act of surrender. In the spirit of the Ignatian Suscipe, I pray "Take Lord; receive." I empty myself of all pretense. I ask God to take and receive any joy or sorrow I might be experiencing today.

I ask God to take and receive my dreams and my fears. I give myself to God just as I am.

Contrition

Within each of us, there is sorrow for the times we have not lived according to God's standards or the standards we set for ourselves. Although many of us are harsh on ourselves and usually expect far more of ourselves than God does, contrition is a key movement in daily prayer.

Contrition invites us to think about our relationships, our mistakes, and our sins. We tell God that we are sorry. Contrition is salutary. It is life-giving and necessary. Contrition softens our hardness and stifles our hubris. We all need to find the strength to say, "I'm sorry."

God's love for us

In this fourth moment of prayer, we are asked to reflect on the fact that God really does care for us. Many priests find it hard to accept this simple fact. One of my greatest surprises as I travel throughout the country giving retreats for priests is that fact that many priests do not think much of themselves. In reality, many priests think little of themselves. Verse after verse of scripture reminds us just how precious each of us is in the eyes of God. To paraphrase Jeremiah 3:13, "I have loved each of you with an everlasting love. I have called you and you are mine."

Petition

We petition and ask God for patience with people and events of our life. We ask God for patience in our ministry as we come to grips with the fact that the demands made of us are many. We ask for patience as we encounter moments of boredom in ministry and its sometimes-monotonous routine. We petition and ask God to attend to the needs of family, friends, and parishioners who have asked us to remember them in our prayers.

We also ask for perseverance and joy. The last thing we want to become are grumpy old priests who seem unhappy. We ask God to gift us with a childlike joy. We ask God to keep us faithful to promises made on the day of our ordination.

Thanksgiving

The most enjoyable and congenial people I encounter in life and ministry are people whose lives are characterized by an "attitude of gratitude." These people lift up our spirits and make us feel good about ourselves. Some of these people have learned gratitude from their own families. Others have learned to be grateful simply by practicing gratitude day in and day out. Others come to gratitude through faith. Regardless of its source, gratitude is a virtue that informs our words and deeds. Gratitude is an essential movement/posture in the daily prayer of busy priests.

To conclude: There are many priests who do incredibly good work but lack inner peace. In most cases, this lack of inner peace can be attributed to a prayer life that is virtually non-existent. A conscious effort each day to enter into the six movements/postures in prayer I have just described is almost always the antidote.

How long do we engage in the type of prayer I have just described?

I suggest we go no longer than 10 minutes. We do not need to force this type of prayer. If, on occasion, I sense a desire to go longer, I go longer. Whenever I experience this desire to go longer in prayer, it usually means I have experienced some new awakening or have been overcome by a feeling of inner peace.

As priests, countless memories and experiences have shaped and formed us. Collectively, these memories and experiences inform what I like to call "priestcraft," which I define as that innate sense that tells us what to do and say at the right time and for the right reason.

I live near a magnificent park of hundreds of acres where people walk, briskly jog, or bicycle every day for exercise. They seem focused, determined, and committed to one salutary mission: to get and remain healthy. Many have Walkmans to stimulate mind and soul as the body pumps out adrenaline and energy. They think, they plan, they remember and ponder as body and spirit join in a concert of commitment to fitness. These people use valuable time in their day for what they believe is essential to their wellbeing.

As I walk the park and see so many people jogging or walking, I often wonder what they are thinking about. What are their hopes and fears? What significant relationships give meaning to their lives?

I ask a similar question as I look at you, my brother priests. What are your hopes and fears? What significant relationships give meaning to your life? Do you believe that you are good and make a valuable contribution to our world and Church?

I do not need to know the answer to these questions, but you do.

If I leave you with anything today, I leave you my firm conviction that the six movements/postures in prayer we have explored will help us name our hopes and fears and make us holier and happy priests.

Liturgy of Christian Burial—Nora Brosnan Crean

Hugh delivered this homily on the occasion of his mother's funeral Mass. The Mass was celebrated in 1992 in Saint Mary's Church in Westfield, Massachusetts.

AS A PRIEST, I have preached many homilies.

Without a doubt, this is the most difficult of all.

In my family's name I welcome Bishop Marshall, the many priests and sisters gathered here today, along with relatives and friends of our dear mother, Nora Brosnan Crean.

Our mother would be proud of her grandsons as pallbearers and her granddaughters enfolding the casket with the liturgical garment with such love. I welcome Nora's friends from her Belmont Street years and Western Circle. I also welcome neighbors at Baystate Place and her wonderful caregivers from Mount Saint Vincent where she spent the last eight months. Our mother would be humbled by the wonderful turnout. At the same time, she would love it!

We gather in this church of Saint Mary's where my mother and father worshiped when they came from Ireland, where they were married sixty years ago, and where all of us were baptized, schooled, and formed in the faith. This is a very sacred place for our family and today is a very sad day because we reluctantly give back to God a very special gift that God so generously gave us.

Yet, our sadness is softened by grateful memories!

Nora came to Westfield to Uncle Dennis from Farranfore, County Kerry, as a young woman of 18. She was bursting with life, optimism, and hope. As with so many of her generation, there were mixed emotions as Nora left behind her parents, two brothers, and three sisters.

In Westfield, Nora married and began a new life of untiring love for her husband and children. Our mother was the unshakeable center of our family. She was deeply loved by her husband and family. Nora was gentle, generous, and welcoming. She had an abundance of friends of all nationalities and religions. To our knowledge, Nora never had an enemy.

Nora loved music and song. She loved dancing and laughter. She loved fun times and fun people. Nora loved both of her countries: Ireland and the United States.

Nora cooked, baked, cleaned, and sang in the kitchen of our family home. Our house was always full. There was Sheila, Jack, Bill, and me. There were the cousins who came one after another to begin their life in America in our family home on 19 Belmont Street. Joe, Jack, Rosemary, Gerry Murphy, Margaret Brosnan, Eileen and Mary Crean, along with Mary Sullivan all called our home their home.

Nora's love eventually grew to include the spouses of her children: Pat, Joan, Herb, Bob, Marcia, and Chet. We believe God gave us the very best when he gave us our mother. For this, we are eternally grateful.

All families have their ups and downs. There were times in our family when sadness and loss seemed overpowering. The premature death of Jack at age 33 was a terrible blow. What sustained Nora was her strong faith in God and God's Providence.

Today's readings were chosen with great care. Biblical wisdom tells us to "seek first the Kingdom of God." Our mother based her life on values and things that really mattered. Prayer, gratitude, and a search for wisdom were her sure foundation. Nora found wisdom in the Church. The Eucharist, the Rosary, and silent prayer meant much to her.

Education meant everything to our parents. They sent us to private colleges at no little cost, sacrificing so that we could have advantages they did not have. For this, dear Nora, we are grateful.

In recent years, our mother's affection lay in her grandchildren, whom she loved and cherished with maternal pride. Our mother had a special love for each of them. She spoke with great pride of their accomplishments.

As our mother's health began to diminish more and more, she and I would talk about death and the hereafter. In many of those conversations, I would take her on a tour of heaven. As part of that tour, we would walk the corridors of heaven and visit my father, all of my mother's dear family, and cherished friends. I would assure her that in heaven she and my dad could go out for a Sunday drive or ride on the back of the ice cream truck as she did as a young wife. I told her that in heaven she could have a cup of tea with special friends or go on another cruise with Sister Thomasine. Nora took special delight when I told her that in heaven she could hug her son Jack again. During those imaginary tours of heaven, my mother would laugh and cry. She would hold my hand and say, "That will be lovely."

Today is not only a day of memory. It is a day of promise. Saint John of the Cross tells us that, "In the evening of life we shall be examined by love." Nora found great solace in these words of Saint John of the Cross. These words animated her entire life of doing good in simple and unassuming ways.

Nora loved the ocean. She left Farranfore many years ago with tearful goodbyes. At the same time, she knew that a new and better life awaited her on the other side of the ocean. In a similar way, we share tears of goodbye today. At the same time, we know that a new and better life awaits our mother on the other side of death.

And so, we give her back this day to the God who says, "Come home to the other shore. Your journey is over. Let my home be your home."

Thanks, Mom, from all of us!

Continue to guide and inspire us from your place of sweet release!

First Mass—Father Christopher Connelly

Hugh delivered this homily in Sacred Heart Church in Springfield, Massachusetts, in 1993. As a seminarian, Father Connelly spent the summer of 1992 as an intern in Sacred Heart Parish. For many years, these two outstanding priests served together on diocesan commissions and boards.

IT IS VERY easy to understand the pride and happiness of this congregation as we celebrate Chris Connelly's First Mass. We congratulate Chris's parents, Carolyn and Bob, his brother Danny, his aunts, uncles, relatives, and friends who have supported him in his journey to the priesthood. It seems like only yesterday that Chris talked to Father George and me about the seminary. Both George and I are proud to stand with Chris today around this altar in Sacred Heart Church.

Recently, I read a commentary by a college student who told friends that his brother was going to be ordained a priest. His college friends asked in return, "Isn't it strange that your brother is becoming a priest?"

We can assume that these college students—like so many in our world—picture the event of ordination and the life of a priest through the critical lens of Freud, Marx, Darwin, and Sagan. They most likely consider the life of a priest as strange and outdated. They see priesthood as daily formal prayer, cultic ritual, black clothing, living where you work, enforced celibacy, minimum salary, at least 21 years of formal education, high expectations of the Church and people you serve, obedience, and constant availability.

Yes, we can see why the life of a priest seems strange to many. Yet, when we consider that fact that in the dictionary definition of "strange," we find "extraordinary" listed as its synonym, we can say that priesthood is extraordinary.

Priesthood is extraordinary insofar it invites priests to work a little harder and to reach a little higher, spurred on by the haunting words they hear at ordination: "Believe what you read; teach what you believe; practice what you teach." Like the mystery of the Holy Trinity which we celebrate today, priesthood seems strange and extraordinary.

If one looks at the glaring headlines portraying the human foibles of priests, one would say it is an especially difficult time to be a priest. However, if one looks at the opportunities to preach, to minister to the young, to comfort the sick, one would say it is an especially wonderful time to be a priest.

Today we celebrate men like Chris who see the precious value of the priesthood and who, with good intentions, seek to live their priesthood the best they can.

On this beautiful afternoon of celebration, we embrace you, Chris. We offer our thanks, our support, and welcome to the presbyterate of the Diocese of Springfield.

What do we know about Chris?

There are the obvious facts of his life we all know. Chris graduated from Cathedral High School, Wilbraham & Monson Academy, Providence College, and Saint John's Seminary. His family shared with him the gift of faith. They have been a constant source of encouragement and have provided a wonderful example of service to others. On this special day, we realize that a vocation is not taught. Rather, it springs forth from the mystery of God's choosing and is nurtured in a family which affirms that service of God and ministry in the Church are both good and honorable.

Not so obvious to many is the fact that Chris is an accomplished organist. He has a great sense of humor. (He needed a good sense of humor to work with Father George and me last year at Sacred Heart and will need a good sense of humor as he undertakes his first assignment in just two weeks!) Chris does not take himself too seriously—a wonderful trait for effective ministry! He is competent, compassionate, and at ease with people of all ages. He is willing to work, willing to learn, and is now ready to get started. Gifted with considerable skills, intelligence, and personality, Chris will be an asset to any parish.

Today, Chris, you begin.

The Lord will use your God-given talents and engaging personality to heal, to love, and to guide. He will use your heart to console and your mind to instruct. You were ordained yesterday by Bishop Marshall but will become a priest through people and events that will shape and form you in the days and years that lie ahead. Know that you are not alone. You will have our love and support as you continue to be shaped and formed through your ministry in our midst.

Four years ago, you responded to a call from God. I can assure you that there will be challenges ahead. I can assure you that there will be great satisfaction living and working with people in moments of joy as you officiate at baptisms and weddings. I assure you that you will know moments of peace as you minister to the sick and the troubled. Finally, I can assure you that you will experience the fun and fraternity of the priesthood.

So, what do we want Father Chris to remember?

Karl Rahner, a wise old priest and respected theologian, says it best:

> The priest is not an angel sent from heaven. He is a man chosen from among others, a member of the Church, a Christian. As one of us and as a Christian, he begins to speak to you the Word of God—and this Word is not his own. No, he comes to you because God has told him to proclaim God's word. Perhaps he has not entirely understood it himself, but he believes. Despite all his fears he knows that he must communicate God's word to you. For must not someone say something about God, about eternal life, about the majesty of grace in our lives? Must not someone stand up and speak of sin, of judgment, and of God's tender mercy? So pray for him, carry him, so that he be able to sustain others by bringing them to the mystery of God's love as revealed by Jesus Christ.
>
> —Karl Rahner, "The Faith of the Priest Today," 1965

Liturgy of Christian Burial—William "Bill" Crean

This homily was delivered in Our Lady of Blessed Sacrament Church in Westfield, Massachusetts, on August 26, 1993, on the occasion of the funeral of Hugh's younger brother, Bill Crean.

MY FAMILY AND I are truly humbled and enormously gratified by the genuine outpouring of love and respect for Bill as together we celebrate this Mass of the Resurrection in his parish church. The presence of our bishops, my brother priests, relatives, and friends is appreciated. The kind words, the sensitive gestures and expression of love and sympathy expressed by all of you mean so much to Pat, Bill, Kelly, Hugh, Jerry, Kevin, Sheila, and all Bill's family.

Mixed emotions swirl and tumble within us. As human beings we feel the pain of loss of a thoroughly good husband, father, brother, and friend who brought joy and love to every situation. Yet, as Christians, we believe that life is not ended. We trust that the warm, welcoming embrace of the Father is the joy and fulfillment of all my brother's dreams.

We are saddened that Bill died so young. Yet we find comfort knowing that he lived his life in accord with the Gospel command to love both God and neighbor. We also find comfort in knowing that, just as Jesus' own suffering gave way to new life, Bill's eighteen-month struggle with cancer gives way to the bright and blessed promise of immortality we celebrate in this church, around this altar.

Our readings for today were carefully chosen by Bill's family and friends. In today's gospel we hear the invitation to seek first God's kingdom, to do things God's way, to work hard, and to trust in God's Providence. Bill and Pat took seriously this invitation of Jesus. They did things God's way. They sought God's kingdom. Hard work and trust in God's providence were the touchstone of their life.

Our second reading from Paul's Letter to the Philippians also has special meaning. At many of our family Masses, we heard Bill read the words we heard today: "My prayer is that your love for one another may increase more and more and never stop improving your knowledge and deepening your perception, so that you can always recognize what is best." This was clearly Paul's prayer for all Christians. At the same time, it was Bill and Pat's special prayer for their children, and our prayer for one another.

Our first reading underscores the most fundamental truth of Christian faith: "The souls of the just are in the hands of God, and no torment shall touch them." These words bring consolation and support at a moment like this.

How can I sum up the life of Bill Crean?

Four character traits describe my brother. The first character trait that comes to mind is humility.

One of the highest honors one can receive is the respect, admiration, and affection of one's peers. Bill's family knew that he was special from his earliest days. His special gifts were recognized by those who knew him during his years in college and the military. The Sheriff's Department and many civic and religious organizations recognized Bill's talent. He was acknowledged for his gifts of personality, competence, and goodness.

Yet, as all of us know, Bill always shrugged off praise and diverted the spotlight from himself to someone else. He consistently made others look good and feel important. Bill taught his best lessons by consistent good example. He was always there and always gentle, steady, strong, and humble. It is no coincidence that he worked until four days before he went to the hospital less than a month ago. He was humble enough to believe a day's wage comes from a day's work.

A second character trait that describes Bill is honor. His own good name, personal integrity, and honesty meant much to him. Bill respected the dignity of every human person. He could laugh at himself for his iron will and determination, but no one could get in the way of his high principles and convictions about right and wrong. For Bill, there was only the right way to do things. To call someone honorable sounds stilted and old fashioned. Yet Bill was neither stilted nor old fashioned. He was honorable in the best sense of the term.

But enough of the strictly serious side.

If Bill is most remembered for any one thing, it will be his sense of hospitality. He and Pat enjoyed every chance to be with people at weddings, parties, neighborhood gatherings, and family celebrations. Holidays were special at their home and good fun was always predictable. To go to a party with him required that you plan in advance to be the last to leave. Hospitality speaks of laughter, singing, and lots of fun. It speaks of open welcome and good spirit. With Bill there was always time for one more song, one more dance, one more conversation, and one more person to include. Bill and Pat passed on that gift of hospitality to their children.

The last character trait that describes Bill is holiness. Although holiness is difficult to define, true holiness begins with balance. Bill went to daily Mass whenever possible. Private prayer and impromptu visits to church were part of his life. His work as a parish and community volunteer contributed to his holiness. Bill's holiness exuded conviction, manliness, and grace.

Bill reminded us that holiness is found not only in the monk or cloister, but also in the man who agonizes with the Red Sox, coaches the Patriots from his armchair, tips over a lamp while watching a fatal interception in a Notre Dame or Boston College game, or watching one of the kids get all net on a three pointer in a high school game.

Bill reminded us that holiness is a soft smile of wisdom, a caring look of forgiveness. He showed us that holiness can be found in the laugh wrinkles around the eyes as well as the calluses on the knees. Bill showed us holiness is about courage in sickness, faith in troubled times, generosity in victory, dignity in defeat, gratitude in prosperity, fidelity in relationships, and reverence for the sacred.

Bill's holiness was apparent every time he read to the blind, attended adoration of the Blessed Sacrament at 3:00 AM, bought groceries for the poor, and made sacrifices for his children's college education.

One of the classics in literature is Cervantes' *The Man of La Mancha*. In Don Quixote we recognize a noble, good, and caring man whose spirit swelled with love and for whom friendship was sacred. Don Quixote saw the best in people. He coaxed from them their goodness and acknowledged the dignity of every human person. Don Quixote was an idealist, a visionary, a searcher, a rare and special incarnation of God's love.

In so many ways, Bill was like Don Quixote. Despite a diagnosis of cancer, he was at work every day and attended all his children's activities. Bill still dreamed what some would call an impossible dream of wellness and fought the unbeatable foe of the cancer that consumed him. With faith and dignity, Bill, like Jesus, carried his cross. I believe that this dear man now shares in Jesus' Resurrection.

In a beautiful book entitled *Ireland: A Terrible Beauty,* there is a picture of a man from the wild and rugged coast of West Kerry, where our parents were born. The man stands proud and strong with bright eyes and a beguiling smile. Under the picture, the caption reads, "Have yourself a good look now, for when I'm gone you'll never see the likes of a man like me, again."

Whether we will ever again see the likes of Bill Crean or not, I do not know.

However, I do know that the little brother with whom I shared a bed when we were children grew up to be the finest man I have ever known.

So go home now, Bill, in a sweet and blessed release to the God you knew and loved so well.

Go home with Dad, Mom, and Jack. Meet the saints and martyrs. Join the heavenly banquet and enliven the party. Lead them in a rousing chorus of "Let There Be Peace on Earth."

Go home with our thanks for your life, your love, and your precious gift of friendship.

Saint Patrick's Day Mass

Each year, Sacred Heart Parish hosts a Mass celebrated by the bishop of the Diocese in honor of Saint Patrick. In 1995, Hugh was named marshal of the prestigious Holyoke Saint Patrick's Day Parade. This is the homily Hugh preached at that special Mass.

EACH YEAR THE celebration of Saint Patrick's Day and its flurry of activities brighten the dreary days of late winter with warmth and joy. This annual celebration in honor of Saint Patrick and the festive parade invites us to honor a great saint. At the same time, this annual celebration stirs our memories and reminds us of who we are and from where we came. This month's festivities help us appreciate our Irish heritage and identity.

Most of the time in these Saint Patrick's Day memorials, we look to the past and the history of the Irish people. We reflect with melancholy on the sadness of oppression and forced immigration because of hunger, lack of employment, discrimination, and political strife. We praise the steadfast faith and incredible devotion of our ancestors. We recognize the pride and ambition of the immigrants and the contributions of the Irish patriots.

We honor with gratitude our parents, grandparents, and all those people of another time who came to this country with little education or money, but great hopes for their children. What sustained them was their faith, their Church, and personal commitment to values.

In this season of Irish celebrations, I encourage all of us here today to build upon those foundations. Our greatest gift to our children and to the future of our Church and country is a strong and living faith. Our abiding legacy to those who come after us is a commitment in season and out of season, when convenient and inconvenient, to spiritual values and a generous sharing of our talents to make the Church and our nation strong.

Today, in gratitude, I want to look to the past, but especially to the present and future of Irish Americans. We do not live in the 1840s, 1900s, or even 1960s. Irish Catholics in the United States today are among the best educated, highest paid, and most influential. They have become increasingly visible in government, business, the military, and the professions. There are Irish American Catholic playwrights, writers, scientists, managers, CEOs, lawyers, teachers, and senators. The immigrant sense of social inferiority and insecurity in the secular world is long gone. This is really not a boast, but more a reminder in the scriptural sense that "to whom much has been given, much is expected."

Once we were on the outside looking in at a nation and professions and businesses run by others. Now we share in the management and assume the responsibility that management brings. The children and grandchildren of immigrants are among the best and the brightest. There is an old Irish expression—"You've come a long way from the attic room." In many ways, the Irish American Catholic laity of the United States is a powerful, sophisticated, educated, sleeping giant called to awaken and apply its considerable imagination and creativity to the work of the Church. The laity have what the clergy do not have. Our laity possess skills learned in life and in school. They manifest their talents in the crafts and professions they practice every day.

There is a reason that we begin this day with the Eucharist. In this Eucharist, we listen to the Word and celebrate the Sacrament of Life.

Each Eucharist is a time to remember with fondness, affection, and prayer those who have gone before us. Saint Patrick is one of these giants. Untold devotion and passion stimulated him to plant the seed of faith among the Irish people. Patrick preached and healed. He baptized and encouraged people to live and act as Christ did.

We have much to celebrate, and we do it well and proudly each year on a crisp and windy Sunday afternoon in March. Let our festivities today in Springfield and Sunday in Holyoke continue to express the indomitable spirit of the Irish of yesterday, today, and tomorrow.

Saint Jude Novena

For parishioners of Holy Name Parish in Springfield, Massachusetts, an annual novena in honor of Saint Jude is an important tradition. Hugh delivered this homily in 1995 while serving as pastor of Holy Name Parish.

THE SAINT JUDE Novena is a cherished and blessed tradition here at Holy Name Parish in Springfield. It is an experience of deep faith and prayer. It is a special time for our parish and for all of us:

- to ask God tenderly for what we need;
- to thank God graciously for what we have received; and
- to seek God's wisdom for all that lies ahead in our journey toward the Kingdom.

You are people of faith. I know you well and love you with affection, trust, and confidence in God's mercy and care. Please believe it. Stay that way in good times and in bad because God listens. God tenderly answers and gently guides those who talk to Him in quiet conversation and prayerful, heartfelt simplicity. That is the essence of our faith.

Prayer is not complicated. It is the disclosure of our soul, the sharing of the heart. Prayer is the sharing of joys and successes for which we are grateful and the problems we are experiencing. Prayer is saying "help me" or "thank you" or "forgive me."

Prayer is also the pain, the jagged edges, and even the questions and doubts we have about life, faith, and the personal issues that effect, distract, and confuse us. I know God is listening and wants a conversation with each of us. May I suggest that you begin your prayer by listening to God's question: "How are you today?" Then, open your heart and unfold and unwrap the package that is you! God wants to hear:

- not how you were yesterday;
- not how you will be in your imagined tomorrow; but

- how you are today, right now, with your present situation, your successes, failures, hopes, dreams, disappointments, and distresses.

If you listen, God will come, and a quiet voice will echo inside you when he says, "I love you. I created you as a unique, unrepeatable act of my creation. There is no one else like you in the world. I know and love you as my own."

This has always been my image of God, and I share it as an image that has sustained me in my life and my almost 50 years of priesthood.

This Saint Jude Novena is similar to a novena so many of us grew up with—the Saint Francis Novena. On a personal note, ironically, I was born 70 plus years ago during the Saint Francis Novena. My birth was touch and go and not easy. My mother prayed to Francis Xavier, and I was born with some complications, but healthy. Francis is my saint, my middle name, and my friend.

Tonight, as you conclude this Saint Jude Novena, take Saint Jude into your heart. Welcome Saint Jude to your soul. Talk to him about your needs. Embrace him with your faith. Cultivate him as your friend, and share him with your family.

A few short days of a parish novena out of 365 days in a year is not much. One hour a day out of 24 hours is not much.

Although the time we spend at this annual novena might not be much, God might just give us more than we could ever ask or imagine.

God loves people of humility, faith, and trust.

God is here with open arms of embrace to all of you.

Believe and trust.

With God, walk the journey to the place He will show you along the way.

Our faith is a gift.

Treasure it.

Open your hearts and let God in.

This is my fervent prayer for each of you during this novena!

A Letter to His Nephew

Hugh wrote this letter in 1996 to his nephew, Michael Crean. Michael was born three months after the death of his father, Jack Crean. Jack Crean was Hugh's oldest brother. At the time of Jack's death in 1968, his other five children were all seven years of age and younger.

Dear Michael,

After 28 years, I want to write to you about your father. I only knew him for 31 years, and most of those years we were just young kids growing up in a very loving home with our parents, immediate family, and lots of cousins who lived and shared their lives with us.

Jack was my older brother by two years. As the oldest son, he was very close to my father and mother. He was warm, loving, intelligent, and popular. He was a little wild and quite spiritual (an interesting combination). In school, Jack was very bright, but did not always work at it. Studies came easily to him and he got by without a lot of effort. Nonetheless, Jack was motivated to succeed. My parents—your grandparents—made us think that nothing was impossible.

Our family did not have a lot of money, but as kids we did not know that. As a boy, Jack was very interested in sports and was a leader among other kids. As he grew older, the beginnings of diabetes began to affect him, although he did not have the real diagnosis until he was 17.

With the diagnosis, things became serious. Jack had to take the insulin needle every day and sometimes twice a day until he died. In his junior year, he had to stay home for most of a semester because of diabetes. Yet, he went back for final exams and made the dean's list. As I said, studies came naturally to Jack. His mind was quick and agile. He was a business major, and after college graduation from Saint Michael's in 1956, he got a job with Hamilton Standard and then National Blank Book in Holyoke.

My brother had been dating your mother for several years, and they were married on Thanksgiving Day, November 24, 1959. Jack was 24, Joan was 23, and their first apartment was on Franklin Street in Westfield. Their first child,

Hugh, was born September 2, 1960, and their family began. Ann followed on September 7, 1961.

During our growing up years, Jack was very close to our parents, both my father and my mother. He was very loving and affectionate to both of them, and they to him. After Jack contracted diabetes, my father had become very tender and protective of him.

My parents were crazy about their new grandkids. They saw Jack, Joan, and the children very often. I was in Baltimore studying at Saint Mary's Seminary during those years. Because of the strict seminary schedule, I was unable to attend your parents' wedding. Only during summer vacations from the seminary did I have a chance to spend time with your parents and you.

In 1962, your father felt it important to go to graduate school for his career. Your entire family went to Chicago where Jack enrolled in the MBA program at Northwestern. Noreen was born in Chicago in May of 1963.

When Jack completed his MBA, your family came back to Holyoke and lived in an apartment in Holyoke. Jack began working for the U.S. Envelope Company. The family continued to grow. Mark was born in 1965.

Life was busy for Jack and Joan. Jack's health was still precarious. He was working hard, but not really taking good care of his diabetes. He was a good father and Joan was a good mother. There were the usual tensions associated with raising a young family, but your parents put together enough money to buy a house on 52 Dorwin Drive in West Springfield. This was also the time that Jack, always a risk taker, became fascinated with the emerging technology of computers. He saw the future of this genius invention, understood its technology, and was convinced of its place in modern society.

Jack was driven to succeed, and I sense that he felt he did not have a lot of time. At this time, he began thinking about leaving U.S. Envelope and starting his own business when along came John in September 1967, the fifth child.

His plan to start the business became a reality when— at great risk—Jack, the brains, and Hal White, the salesman, left U.S. Envelope in 1968 and founded a company they called Administrative Systems, Inc. There was a feverish period of organization and development that consumed his time and energy. A giant mind and a frail body were competing against each other as Jack made inroads in this new industry of computer technology.

At about this time, Joan became pregnant again. With Hugh only 7½ years old, and a sixth child on the way, life was really hectic for Jack and Joan.

Summer and autumn of 1968 were, in my memory, great seasons for our family. Your uncle Bill and his new wife, Pat, had an apartment in Lee. Pat and Joan were both expecting babies. The children were beautiful, healthy, and full of fun—and life giving to all of us. I was in my sixth year at Saint Michael's, East Longmeadow, and knew that I was going to Europe in 1969 for doctoral studies. Your aunt, Sheila, was in her 17th year as a Sister of St. Joseph and teaching at Saint Mary's School in Longmeadow.

I still remember Thanksgiving Day 1968. Jack, Bill, and I went to the annual Cathedral-Westfield football game. We took the kids. I had your brother, Mark, on my shoulders most of the time. The Thanksgiving "party" was wonderful. I remember thinking to myself, "It doesn't get much better than this."

In early December, a very strong Asian flu swept across the country. Usually nobody pays much attention to the seasonal flu. Jack got the flu, and everyone thought it was no big deal. He was home from work, sick to his stomach, vomiting.

On December 12th, your father suddenly fell into a coma. Joan called me. I came to West Springfield. Jack was taken by ambulance to the hospital. By the time I arrived at the hospital with your mother, your father had died.

Without warning, the bright light of Jack's heart, mind, and spirit had been so quickly extinguished.

The family was in shock and mourning. In fact, all of Westfield felt the pain of losing such a young man. What especially hurt was the sight of a young mother, six months pregnant with five little children and the realization that their father, Jack, would never see the baby yet to be born in three months.

Those days following your father's death were hard. On March 28, 1969, I drove your mom to the hospital. I waited patiently with her until you were born later that day with your father looking on from heaven. Your mother named you "Michael." You and your brother, John, never knew your father; Mark and Norine have vague memories of your father. Ann and Hugh have distinct, but faded memories as seven- and eight-year-olds at the time of your father's death.

Who was your father?

He was my older brother. He was beautiful as a child. As an adult, he was intelligent and generous. Your father was a party person and a risk taker. At the same time, he was deeply spiritual, personable, caring, and loving. He had a mind for business and was a courageous dreamer.

I loved and admired your father. I always thought that, together, we would share a long life. Your mother is fortunate in so many ways. Having lost her first husband, she found Herb Pavel. All of you children are also fortunate to have your mother and the warm, caring, faithful, and tender love and guidance of Herb.

Life goes on. There are few days when I do not remember my parents and my brothers, Jack and Bill. But I still have you, Michael, your brothers, sisters, and cousins.

I miss your father, but I am eternally grateful that he lived. I am grateful that your mother and your father had you and that you are my nephew and my friend.

I love you,
Hugh

Liturgy of Christian Burial— Father Cyril Burns

Hugh was frequently invited to deliver the homily at funeral Masses honoring his brother-priests. Father Cyril (Cy) Burns was one of Hugh's close friends. This homily was delivered in 1998 in Saint Theresa's Church in South Hadley, Massachusetts, where Cy was a beloved pastor.

THE LAST TIME I stood in this pulpit was two years ago. It was for a happy celebration in honor of your pastor and friend's 40th anniversary of priesthood. The Mass was festive. The celebration at The Wherehouse? was joyous. Most of us here today were part of those celebrations.

Today, we gather once again as friends and family. We remember our priest and our friend with love, gratitude, and prayer as we give him back to God. We honor Cy's humanity, his goodness, his faith, and his courage.

In a little-known speech, W.B. Yeats asks: "Why should we honor those that die upon the field of battle? A man may show as reckless a courage in entering into the abyss of himself."

Cy Burns did not embark on any military field of battle. Yet, for many years, he demonstrated a reckless and defiant courage as he battled the scourge of cancer and countless surgeries. Cy may have lost his battle with cancer, but we firmly believe that he now shares in the Easter victory over death that we celebrate this season.

Cy's journey began long ago just a few miles from here. The only son of Christopher and Mary Alice Burns, Cy grew up and was educated in Saint Jerome Parish, Holyoke. He played ball and walked that city's streets and parks with many of his lifelong friends here today before going off to Saint Francis College in Pennsylvania and then to Saint Mary's Seminary in Baltimore.

Father Burns had the distinction of serving as a priest in all four counties of our Diocese. He was assigned to parishes in Greenfield, Huntington, Easthampton, Dalton, North Adams, Belchertown, and Palmer. He served as pastor of Holy Family in Springfield and here at Saint Theresa's for 17 years. Although this listing of parishes might seem impressive, it does not tell us much about the man except that he was incredibly adaptable. Cy got along well with people and was graciously responsive to the bishop's call whenever that call came. Wherever he went, Cy was quickly loved by parishioners.

There are three characteristics that describe Cy's life and witness for me.

The first is *holy*. That might surprise you. We all know that Cy was not pious or churchy. But beneath the "regular guy" exterior was the wonderful beauty of a holy man. Real holiness means a solid faith in God, fidelity to promises, hope in adversity, being present to people's needs, and reliance on God's plan. These virtues characterized my friend Cy Burns, whether he was celebrating Mass, visiting the hospital, in the confessional, or at the home of a parishioner or friend.

Secondly, he was *human*. Cy was almost always upbeat. He loved a good joke, a good story, a good party, and a good time. He was always good fun. He could laugh with others because he had learned to laugh at himself. From his earliest days, Cy shared that humanity with friends like Father Tony Creane and Father Jim Flahive every Tuesday night. He shared that humanity with Father Matt O'Connor, Father Peter Loughran, Norman, Eddie, and other friends from Holyoke and South Hadley. He shared that humanity with the many Sisters of St. Joseph and families he met along the way.

Cy's humanity showed itself in his tendency to exaggerate. A magnificent putt in a game of golf got longer and longer with each telling. The rigors of the seminary and his assignments with tough pastors became epic in proportion. His humanity also showed itself in his willingness to forgive and his hesitancy to criticize others. Cy's humanity brought out the best of what it is to be human in each of us. He was good company.

Thirdly, Cy was *humble*. Like the other two virtues we have described, humility found singular expression in Cy Burns. Few of us have endured the painful and humiliating health problems that Cy experienced as a victim of facial cancer. He bore these multiple surgeries and humiliations without complaint. He never caved in. Cy was blessed with an incredible ability to endure with faith, courage, and humility.

There is an exquisite beauty in Cy's kind of humility. He was humbled by the adversity of cancer but never overcome. During this latest painful and fatal crisis, he kept the faith. Cy wanted only to put parish and personal business in order and then leave the rest to God. For this, Cy has my unending admiration.

Our reading tonight is from Saint Paul's letter to Timothy: "I have fought the good fight. I have kept the faith."

These words are most appropriate as we celebrate the life of our pastor and friend, Father Cyril Burns.

Cy stayed to the task, he fought the fight, he kept the faith.

I truly believe that Cy now experiences the joys of God's Kingdom, where all lost things are found, broken things are mended, and every good thing for which we have hoped is eternally ours.

May Cy's holy, human, and humble soul rest in peace.

Farewell Mass

Following nearly seven years as pastor of Holy Name Parish in Springfield, Massachusetts, Hugh was reassigned in 1999 to Our Lady of the Blessed Sacrament Parish in Westfield, Massachusetts. Hugh delivered this homily in conjunction with a celebration honoring his years of service at Holy Name Parish.

AFTER SIX AND a half years as your pastor, I have been transferred from Holy Name Parish to a new assignment as pastor of Blessed Sacrament Parish in Westfield. I am leaving Holy Name with nothing but good memories of very good people and very fulfilling ministry. I love this city, this parish, and its parishioners. This assignment has been a challenge I enjoyed and an experience I will always treasure.

Why is this happening now?

Let me assure you that the bishop did not send me away! I am almost 62 years old and have been a priest for 37 years. With the shortage of clergy, I remain very involved in diocesan work and assume the responsibilities that come with that work. Lay ministry formation, personnel management, and the Future of Faith initiative absorb much of my time. I am involved in the National Institute for Clergy Formation and facilitate retreats for priests throughout the country. These programs and initiatives demand considerable time and energy. As a result, I have asked to be assigned to a smaller parish.

I have been assigned to only three parishes: Saint Michael's in East Longmeadow, Sacred Heart in Springfield, and Holy Name in Springfield. I have left each of these assignments with a heavy heart. (I guess you could say that I'm an emotional Irishman!)

The energy and goodness of Holy Name Parish flows in my bloodstream. Holy Name is a vibrant parish, a loving parish, a down-to-earth parish. Holy Name parish is a diverse parish. Holy Name is alive with kids, vitality, lots of day-to-day activities, and excitement.

We have a staff of competent and good people. We have teachers, coaches, and mentors. We have solid buildings and programs. In an uncertain world, we have some financial stability. Most of all, we have a future full of promise.

I have always insisted that, although ordained by a bishop, priests become priests by the example and witness of the people to whom we are sent. These same people form and shape us. They make us priests.

Whether preaching, baptizing, officiating at weddings, or presiding over funerals, I have enjoyed being your priest. I have enjoyed seeing you at parish functions and meetings. I have enjoyed chatting with you after Mass. You, the people of Holy Name, have formed me, encouraged me, and challenged me as a person and as a priest.

I sincerely thank you for allowing me to be your pastor. Please remember me and pray for me, as I will remember and pray for you.

Twenty years ago today, I was appointed co-pastor with Father George Farland of Sacred Heart Parish. I left Sacred Heart in 1992 to come to Holy Name. Leaving Sacred Heart to come here was difficult. Leaving Holy Name to go to Westfield is just as difficult.

In going to Westfield, I return to my home and to a parish in which my mother, newly arrived from Ireland, was first received and welcomed into this country. Perhaps I can extend to others the same warm welcome my mother received. This is my humble hope and fervent desire.

Please pray for me, as I pray for you.

Know that I will never forget the lessons and kindness I have received from the wonderful people of Holy Name.

Thank you.

Bless you, the wonderful people of this parish, for teaching me to be a priest.

100th Anniversary—Saint Mary's School

Hugh delivered this homily in 1999 in conjunction with the 100th anniversary of his alma mater, Saint Mary's School. The occasion also celebrated the 50th anniversary of the high school Class of 1949.

IN HIS ELOQUENT introduction to the centennial yearbook, Father Tony Creane wrote that a very lovely lady, Saint Mary, gave birth to more than 3,500 young men and women who shared her life and values on the unpretentious corner of Bartlett and Mechanic Streets at Saint Mary's School.

Tonight, I feel honored and privileged to represent all of you and those hundreds of graduates of Saint Mary's Grammar and High Schools on this day of happy celebration.

We are here tonight to remember the modest and simple beginning. We are here to think of the good and gracious people of Saint Mary's past. We are here to thank the nuns, priests, parishioners, and lay teachers who made and continue to make it possible to celebrate the gift that Saint Mary's has been to all of us.

A whole collage of images swirls in my head as I remember:

- Minstrel shows and class plays;
- Father Dowd distributing boxes of hard candy at Christmas to grammar school kids;
- Herlihy and Casey milk bottles sitting in the sun and waiting for us at recess;
- Champs and Rastas, Landeau's, Eatons, the Park and the Strand, May processions, collections for Chinese babies, being referred to as "Master" or "Miss" and never by a nickname;
- Friday night dances with Ed Connelly, Father D., and Mr. Egan;
- The always courageous, giving, and inspiring Ed Courtney, who coached grammar school kids learning to play basketball from his wheelchair;
- Happy Houlihan, Mondo, Tom Courtney, Joe Keefe, Bill Bullens, and all the wonderful coaches and teachers who received little pay for great effort;
- 12 rooms for 12 grades and one all-purpose chemistry lab.

In these 100 years, we had pastors named Donohue, Fitzgerald, Curran, Kirby, Dowd, Shea, Scanlon, Creane, and Tatro. They were founders, builders, sustainers, and saviors.

There were the native sons ordained as priests and the curates, too. These are too numerous to name, but each of these men is remembered in some grateful kid's heart. Their names were Donohue, Burke, Reilly, O'Neil, Johnson, Joyce, and Crowley; Walsh, O'Connor, Quigley, Decoteau, McDonnell, and Carberry; Flahive, Noiseau, Devine, and Griffin; Bernier, Caron, Martin, and Murphy; Foley, Wallis, Lavelle, Lynch, and Lisowski; Salatino, Savage, and Sipitkowski. They were tall and short, older and younger. These great men we knew and respected.

As great as these priests might have been, we all know that from the beginning the heart and soul of Saint Mary's School has been the Sisters of St. Joseph and the lay teachers who worked with them.

Who can forget Sister Thomasine?

Sister Thomasine operated from the powerhouse that was her office but was everywhere in the building. She would burst into classrooms saying, "Be builders and not destroyers." She ran the school like a ship's captain for 30 years, coaxing excellence, expecting learning, and settling for nothing less than everyone's best effort as we sneaked up on the mystery of adulthood.

Other principals followed Sister Thomasine: Sisters Vincent Clare, Agnes Dolores, Clare Edward, and Mary Lavelle; Sisters Quinlan, Broughan, Sheehan, and Griffin; Sisters Marrin, McKiernan, Lavoie, Methe, and Gilbert. Then came our lay principals: Lane, Kapinos, and now Paul Romani, a graduate and hometown boy.

The teachers who taught us were enormously influential in our education and our lives. Names like Fidelis, Andy, Helen, Regina, Ann Teresa, Patty James, Joseph Paul, Marita, Flavia, Christopher, Casper; David, Catherine, Marie, and Josephine all hold a special place in our hearts.

These Sisters and so many others made school an occasion to ponder and dream about our vocation. Future lawyers and salespersons, typists and teachers found their start right here at Saint Mary's.

Sisters of St. Joseph like Joan Schneider and Gil, along with dedicated lay teachers who serve our school today, walk in the same company and share the spotlight of the Sisters who preceded them.

Great supporters named Allen, O'Brien, Tucker, Flahive, and many others contributed time and money for Saint Mary's School.

A former curate, Leo O'Neil, served our Diocese as auxiliary bishop

A graduate of Saint Mary's, Sister Jane Morrissey, is president of her religious congregation.

Legislators, secretaries, teachers, coaches, mothers, fathers, workers, and leaders learned to read, count, think, and contribute on the corner of Bartlett and Mechanic Streets.

How did it all begin?

One hundred years ago, with 150 students and five Sisters of St. Joseph, Saint Mary's School was born. From that time on, the Sisters of St. Joseph and lay teachers who later joined them have brought their dedication to Catholic education, concern for students, and sense of mission to their work here at Saint Mary's School. The hallowed classrooms, halls, and schoolyard still speak volumes to us as our memories wander back to a gentler, freer time.

Saint Mary's is a school about children. Saint Mary's is a school about you when you were younger and you were here—the same holds true today. Saint Mary's School is still about the laughter, innocence, and carefree spirit of kids.

A school is a house of formation, a tradition maker, a value center, a memory bank. A Catholic school is a sanctuary, a home, a family. It is a place where not only math and science and literature are taught, but also values and virtues. A Catholic school is about God and Jesus Christ. It is about the Gospel and faith. A Catholic school is about human rights and values.

A long time ago, President Lincoln said, "A child of today is a person who will carry on what we have started." Lincoln went on to say, "A child will sit where you are sitting and, when you are gone, will attend to those things which you think are important."

Our parish school still lives on. It is a force for good in the City of Westfield and a sign of home to the Diocese of Springfield. Saint Mary's School carries on the things we think are important.

How does a small parish school—especially a high school—endure in an era characterized by limited subsidies, tuition, and a fierce competition for students?

A school like Saint Mary's endures:

- By a conviction that our school is valuable and has something to contribute to our world and Church;
- By imagination on the part of parents and the parishes to promote excellence and keep education affordable and life-giving;
- By a determination and faith that Christian values, sacrifice, and dedication in the formative years of our kids' lives will frame and support their choices for a lifetime;
- By faith in the task itself and a belief that the message of a carpenter from Nazareth still has something to say to kids today.

In thanksgiving for the past and with great hope for the future that is ours, I want to:

- Praise the Sisters of St. Joseph who, from the beginning, worked for a pittance out of a religious commitment to our parish children;
- Praise our lay teachers and the Sisters of today who believe in what they do and who support their families and religious congregation on very small salaries because they know this school is special;
- Praise this parish of Saint Mary's, which continues to support the school in good times and bad and thus keeps the tradition of Catholic education alive in this City of Westfield.

Tonight, in the company of Nellie Roache, our legendary first graduate, and more than 3,500 others who have walked through the doors of Saint Mary's School, I want all of us to toast our past, to pray for our future, and to enjoy this evening of glad celebration.

Liturgy of Christian Burial— Father John Johnson

As a curate (associate) assigned early in his priesthood to Hugh's home parish, John "Johnny" Johnson greatly influenced Hugh's decision to study for the priesthood. The two became lifelong friends. Hugh delivered this homily in 2001.

LONG AGO, A priest celebrated his first Mass on the day following his ordination. This first Mass took place in a priest's home parish. The newly ordained priest would choose two priests he knew and liked to serve with him as deacon and subdeacon.

My first Mass was celebrated in Saint Mary's Church in Westfield. The deacon for that Mass was my parish priest, Father John Johnson. I knew him when I was a kid. I respected and admired him.

From the day of that first Mass on, John—now a brother priest—became my mentor, advisor, counselor, and consoler.

John introduced me to priesthood. As our friendship grew, we became a source of mutual support for each other. For 40 years, John shared my journey, and I shared his journey. We shared ideas, hopes, dreams, successes, decisions, and desires. We shared lunch and dinner. We exchanged books.

I shall miss John's bear hug of Cursillo bravado. I shall miss discussing theology with him. I shall miss his corny jokes.

John's journey began in the Hungry Hill section of Springfield. His parents, like mine, had strong Irish and Catholic roots. John attended Our Lady of Hope School and Cathedral High School, both in Springfield. He went on to study at Saint Michael's College and the Grand Seminary in Montreal. As a young priest, he was sent to the North American College in Rome where he earned a doctorate in theology.

In 1956, John established the Marriage Counselling Office. He served for 45 years in that ministry with Jeannie at his side as secretary and friend. John taught at Elms College and in the Sisters of Providence formation program.

John was especially proud of his work with the Priests Senate and was instrumental in establishing support groups for priests. The Friday gatherings he hosted were legendary. I still have a large box or articles sent monthly from John's office to priests of the Diocese. These articles focused on topics helpful in the ongoing formation of clergy and pastoral care of parishioners.

How would I describe John Johnson to someone who never met him?

I would emphasize John's compassion, especially with the needy. As a counselor to people in need, he was caring and courageous in leading others to self-discovery. I would also stress John's intellect and bright mind. He read books of theology as well as books of pastoral counseling and psychology. John enjoyed classical literature as much as he enjoyed contemporary novels. Discussions about spirituality and theology excited him.

Saint Paul tells us that there are three things that last: faith, hope, and love. Paul also tells us that the greatest of these is love.

John loved his parents and brother. He loved Jeannie and Danny. John loved his aunt, Sister Mary Matthew, and his nieces and nephews. He loved his parishioners, clients, Cursillistas, and brother priests. John expressed that love with hugs and words of encouragement.

After a short stay in Holyoke Hospital, John has gone home to God.

And so, as we give John back to God, we do so with a prayer that he find happiness in that place where all things broken are mended, all things lost are found, all things forgotten are remembered, and everything hoped for is ours for all eternity.

May John's good soul and the souls of all the faithful departed rest in peace.

Month's Mind Mass—Monsignor Thomas Devine

Monsignor Thomas "Tom" Devine was assigned to Hugh's home parish during Hugh's childhood years. During his tenure as president of Elms College, Monsignor Devine invited Hugh to join the faculty. This homily was delivered in 2001 in Saint Mary's Church in Longmeadow, Massachusetts, where Monsignor Devine served as pastor.

MONSIGNOR THOMAS DEVINE and I were both born and raised in Westfield. Tom was eighteen years older than me, but in my memory, he was always there. We weren't related by blood, but his cousins were my cousins. Tom was by my side at my First Mass in 1962. Tom was also by my side when my father, my brothers, and my mother died. These deaths were many years apart, but he was always there.

Monsignor Tom Devine and I served together on virtually every committee and commission in the Diocese. Whenever the Priests' Senate, Clergy Commission, Diocesan Consultors, and countless other committees met, he was always there. Whether at the Elms College where Tom and I worked together or in local hospitals, he was always there whenever someone was in need.

I am ordained almost 40 years and never remember a time in the Diocese of Springfield when Tom Devine was not there as a trusted advisor to our bishops and an icon of hope and consolation for God's people. Tom respected persons of all faith traditions and they respected him.

As many of us know, Tom lived for many years at the Providence Motherhouse where he befriended countless Sisters of Providence and the children they cared for in the orphanage at Brightside. He championed Catholic education at all levels. He gave special meaning to the title of "pastor" in Chicopee, in Springfield, and in Longmeadow, which has been his home for the last 22 years.

Nice cars, clothes, and personal comforts meant little to Tom. By contrast, care, consideration, compassion, and Christ-like charity meant everything to Tom. Like Jesus, Tom was a sign of contradiction. He was a monsignor who preferred to be called "Father." Although he himself ate like a Spartan, Tom was a gracious and bountiful host.

Tom Devine loved Saint Mary's Parish and its grammar school. He loved the town of Longmeadow. This parish and this town were his mission. With a well-worn suit and older car, Monsignor Devine was immediately recognized by people of all faiths in Longmeadow and beyond.

There was great fun in Tom. He loved a good joke or story and would giggle like a kid. He loved to needle close friends and family. He did so playfully and never with malice.

With Tom, a raised eyebrow meant that a meeting was going too long. A wisecrack or joke meant that the meeting was getting too heated. A hasty, but gracious, departure meant that the meeting was off-track and had lost its focus.

It is most appropriate that this Memorial Mass be celebrated on a Friday evening. For many years, Tom would meet regularly on Friday nights with a group of priests for conversation and dinner. They met as friends to talk over the events of the week, to share successes and struggles, to enjoy each other's company. Most of these priests are now dead. I like to think that on this Friday night Tom and his friends are reunited, laughing and sharing in God's heavenly kingdom.

Although we will miss this great man and wonderful priest, we take comfort in knowing that he was always there.

Tonight we pray around this altar where Monsignor Tom Francis Devine celebrated Mass so often that God will give his vibrant mind, great soul, and priestly spirit the reward and peace he so well deserves.

Easter Vigil—2002

Each year, Hugh looked forward to Holy Week and the Sacred Triduum. He especially enjoyed celebrating the Easter Vigil. This homily was delivered in Our Lady of the Blessed Sacrament Church in Westfield, Massachusetts, two years prior to Hugh's retirement as pastor.

OUR CEREMONY THIS evening, the most solemn and sacred of all Church rituals, speaks a beautiful story of hope, of life, and of joy to every man, woman, and child.

Jesus Christ, whom the whole world could not contain, was born from the womb of Mary. He lived His life doing good works; was arrested, tried, and put to death. If Jesus' death had been the end of the story, it would be a tragic story.

Fortunately, we know that death was not the end. Jesus broke the bonds of death. The Easter message proclaims that He rose from the dead and is still with us. The Easter message tells us that death can be overcome and that light is stronger than darkness.

Today, we celebrate a very beautiful story.

At the same time, we ask ourselves a question: "Do we believe the story?"

Do we believe that God can make the dead live again? Do we believe that God can bring light out of the darkness of doubt and fear? Do we believe that God's grace is stronger than any sin?

These are the Easter questions.

My dear people, we have such eloquent reasons for faith and hope. Regardless of any darkness caused by any financial, physical, or emotional problems which surround us, the light of Christ shines forth and overcomes all darkness.

As we passed on the light to one another in our opening ceremony, we shared the victory of the Resurrection. We are now invited to share the light of Christ's victory with each other.

In today's Easter gospel, Mary goes to the tomb to anoint a corpse. She hopes to find Jesus among the dead, but instead the living Jesus calls her by name, "Mary."

Today, the living Jesus calls you and me by name. He says, "Do not be afraid. I have risen and am still with you."

May the message of the Risen Christ be our Easter joy and consolation.

Tonight we do not mourn Jesus' death.

We exult in His life and the good news of salvation.

In the name of all of us honored to minister here at Our Lady of the Blessed Sacrament Parish, I wish you all a very Happy and Blessed Easter!

Liturgy of Christian Burial— Sister Helen Elizabeth

In a note written to himself after retirement, Hugh named Sister Helen Elizabeth as his most memorable grammar school teacher. This homily was delivered in 2004 in Mont Marie Chapel. Located in Holyoke, Massachusetts, Mont Marie was once the motherhouse of the Sisters of St. Joseph of Springfield.

THERE IS A DISCERNIBLE respect and deep sense of loss in this chapel as we mourn the death of Sister Helen Elizabeth, who served as a Sister of St. Joseph for 70 years.

I met Sister Helen in her first assignment at Saint Mary's in Westfield. I was seven years old at that time and have never forgotten this great woman. Who could forget her and her wonderful personality?

When I met Sister Helen later in life, long after she left Westfield to teach throughout New England and serve as principal in several schools, I felt the same affection and gratitude I first felt as a second grader. She still had the enthusiasm of a child and the courage to reach out to anyone who needed her. What a wonderful description of a real disciple of the Lord!

Sister Helen was willing to try most anything with the spirit of mission and adventure. Her exuberance and zest for life, for God, for fun, and for learning were contagious.

She wore her piety with a combination of old-time religion, basic goodness, and practical spirituality. She always wanted to learn, to enjoy God's world, and to share God's blessings in the company of her Sisters and others whom she met on life's journey.

Sister Helen was at home in the convent and with schoolchildren as a teacher and principal. She was equally as comfortable working at Weston Rehab with people in need of care, confidence, or counsel at a troubled time in their lives.

Although possessing all the attention to detail and skill needed to serve as principal of three large schools, Sister Helen loved a party, a good time, a joke, laughter, and fun. In later years, her eyesight was poor, but she never lost her zeal for life, travel, and people.

Sister Helen lived through most of the 20th century. She saw the Church, country, and culture undergo radical changes. She adapted to these many changes with energy and vitality. Rather than choosing to endure these changes with a passive spirit, Sister Helen embraced and internalized new ways of thinking and doing. She flourished in a changing world and a changing Church. This was part of her charm and charisma.

The readings for today help us to see her values. She chose for her funeral gospel the charter of Christian discipleship known as the Beatitudes. "Blessed are the poor in spirit. Blessed are the merciful. Blessed are those who work for what is right. Blessed are the peacemakers. Blessed are the pure of heart."

The Beatitudes define the attributes of Christian life. At the same time, the Beatitudes reflect promises made to those who live by these attributes.

Thank you, Helen, for living these Beatitudes in your own inimitable way.

Let's pray that the family of Sister Helen and the Congregation of Sisters of St. Joseph of Springfield will find comfort in the words of the Anglican priest Henry Scott Holland:

> In death I have only slipped away into the next room. Whatever we were to each other, we still are. Call me by my own familiar name. Laugh as we always laughed together. Play, smile, think of me, and pray for me. Why should I be out of your thoughts because I am out of your sight? I am but waiting around the corner. All is well. Nothing is lost. One brief moment and it will be as it was before—but only better. We will be one together with Christ.

Helen, you taught so many of us what it is to live with disability; to live with intensity; to rejoice in adversity; to prevail with tenacity. You taught us to love with reckless abandon.

May the angels lead you into Paradise. May the martyrs receive you at your arrival and lead you to the holy city Jerusalem. May choirs of angels receive you, and with Lazarus, once a poor man, may you have eternal rest.

Liturgy of Christian Burial— Monsignor John Harrington

Monsignor John Harrington served the Diocese of Springfield with distinction for 69 years as a chancery official and parish priest. John was especially fond of Hugh. The two enjoyed a very special friendship. This homily was delivered in 2004 at Holy Cross Church in Holyoke, Massachusetts.

SISTER NORA AND all members of the Harrington Family:

Today's Liturgy of Christian Burial for your brother, uncle, and cousin began with the words, "We are gathered here in faith, touched by the death of our brother."

Today I have the blessed privilege, even in sadness, of expressing the esteem of all here present—family, friends, parishioners, bishops, priests, and religious sisters—who have been touched by the death of the inimitable Monsignor John Francis Harrington. We are touched by the death of a man who transformed hearts, engaged minds, nourished spirits, and comforted the afflicted.

Monsignor Harrington fed the *hungry* with knowledge stored in his expansive mind. He satisfied the *thirsty* with the consolation of hospitality and welcome at his rectory and office. He attended with goodness and legendary care to the needy who knocked at his rectory door. He looked after the bruised and the sad. He cared for priests, parishioners, and family.

John pondered and labored over decisions. His expressive face and voice spoke eloquently of an inner passion and quest for truth. He always wanted to do the right thing, at the right time, and for the right reasons.

Who was John Harrington?

"Inimitable" is a high-priced word which describes the man we honor today with Christian burial. Surely, there was no one I ever met quite like John Harrington. Sometimes he spoke English like a child sent at an early age to a school in Switzerland. Sprinkled in his conversations were phrases in Latin or French. John was a Renaissance man. He could converse easily about the fate of the Red Sox or the latest international, world, or Church news from the

London Tablet. A rather gruff exterior often hid the laughter of a playful spirit. He loved a good story, a good joke, and a good laugh. Beneath his serious demeanor was a passionate soul, a compassionate heart, and a razor-sharp mind whose hallmarks were intelligence, charity, and graciousness.

To John Harrington, names were names. There were no nicknames. Jim was always James; Jack was John; Tony was Anthony; Joe was Joseph. A phone call from John always ended abruptly with "very well then" followed by a click. With that, the line went dead! How dearly I will miss those phone calls and that click!

John's emotions were quite visible and his mood easily revealed. He had the agonized look of a disappointed father if there was bad news about a priest or the Diocese. He had a broad smile of genuine pride when a successful project was completed.

John loved to preach. He prepared homilies with great care and diligence. Like many of his generation, he wrote his homilies in careful penmanship. His homilies were sprinkled with classical and contemporary allusions. The finished product reflected his considerable education and study. Homilies were delivered in elegant syntax. There were no dangling participles or misplaced metaphors. In the pulpit, John was both engaging and intense.

Direct and forthright in his manner and style, always true to his principles, fair and just in judgements, honest and open in his decisions, John Harrington was the best the Church has to offer in any era.

Cardinal Newman, in *The Idea of a University*, said, "The true gentleman is never mean or little in disputes, never takes unfair advantage, never mistakes personalities or sharp sayings for arguments, or insinuates evil."

This describes the John Harrington we all came to know and love.

This describes the John Harrington we give back to God.

As a priest, Monsignor Harrington was the big brother and cherished friend of Bishop Timothy Harrington of Worcester. Teddy was 10 years younger than John. Teddy's death saddened John and all the Harrington family. His brother Tom and sisters Mary and Margaret also predeceased John.

John's assignments included a brief stay at Saint Patrick's, South Hadley. From there he went on to graduate studies in canon law in Rome. His years in Rome were followed by an uninterrupted period of loyal and distinctive service to

Bishop O'Leary, Bishop Weldon, Bishop Maguire, Bishop O'Neil, Bishop Marshall, Bishop Dupré, and Bishop McDonnell.

During his many years of service in the chancery, John was a road map and a beacon. He served as the Chancellor, Diocesan Consulter, and member of the very first Priests Senate. John was our first Vicar for Clergy, Chairman of the Priests' Personnel Board. For 40 years, he was the Director of the Propagation of the Faith, a ministry he cherished.

John was pastor of Saint Mary's Parish in East Springfield for seven years. He then served for 24 years as pastor of Holy Cross Parish in his beloved native city of Holyoke.

Holyoke meant everything to John. The highlight of his week was Sunday dinner on Walnut Street with his family. Time spent every Sunday with Sister Nora, the love of his life, and Sister Margaret James, her companion, was important to him. John enjoyed a very special relationship with his brothers and sisters, nephews and nieces, Courtney, cousins, and pals form Holyoke.

Marie Wilson who is here today was Monsignor Harrington's secretary, friend, and loyal co-worker for more than 30 years. Marie, please know that he was grateful for your tender care, loving service, and gracious partnerships in ministry.

John cherished his annual trips to the White Mountains in New Hampshire. You could set a clock by John Harrington. He left Holyoke on August 15 and returned Labor Day. He loved to engage with other guests at the hotel, play golf, relax, and celebrate early morning Mass for the caddies before they began their daily work.

John's letters were memorable and charming. Large script with a distinctive flourish expressed tender and caring messages. I, like so many here today, will miss those letters and John's unique impact on our lives.

Ten years ago, during a testimonial to John at the College of the Holy Cross in Worcester where he graduated in 1938, I quoted from Leon Uris.

In Uris's book *Ireland, A Terrible Beauty* is a picture of an older man. The man has bright, flashing, expressive blue eyes and a strong, handsome face with a prominent jaw and proud bearing. The man is standing on the rugged, rocky coast of West Kerry, where Monsignor Harrington's parents were born. Beneath the caption are the words "Have yourself a good look now, for when I'm gone you'll never see the likes of a man like me, again." We probably will never see the likes of John Harrington again. John was one of a kind. He lived a very full life for almost 95 years.

And so we pray:

John, go home to God, where all lost things are found, where all broken things are mended, and where everything you ever hoped for is yours to experience eternally in the company of the God you served so well.

May the angels lead you into Paradise and may the martyrs welcome you to the new and eternal Jerusalem.

Special Anniversaries—Sisters of Providence

Hugh was a friend of many Sisters of Providence. He was an avid supporter of their charism and mission. In retirement, Hugh lived at Providence Place in Holyoke, Massachusetts, where he ministered to the Sisters of Providence and others living in the retirement community. This homily was delivered in 2007.

SEVERAL TIMES A day, I pass by the imposing statue of Mother Mary of Providence that stands just outside our beautiful home. Each time I pass by, I am compelled to stop and ponder.

Stately, confident, faithful, and strong, she stands on the hill beside two young children whose hands she holds in an unspoken embrace which speaks a mission of service, of care, of providence to these children and countless others. This statue reminds those who pass by of this woman's zeal and commitment to use her God-given gifts in the service of God's people, especially the young, the sick, and the poor. The tiny seed planted by Mother Mary of Providence has since flowered into a magnificent garden of splendid service and ministry to thousands of people.

In one way or another, we are all the beneficiaries of the tender and loving ministry of the Sisters of Providence. In a special way, those of us living in the Diocese of Springfield are grateful for the difference these women have made in our life as a local church.

This is not a day for high oratory or elaborate preaching. This is a day to acknowledge with gratitude and simplicity our jubilarians whose life and ministry embody the vision of Mother Mary of Providence and the charisma of the congregation she founded.

We gather to honor those Sisters celebrating 60 years of ministry: Sisters Mary Caritas, Mary Bernadette, Mary Cecilia, Mary Peter, Margaret Kelley, and Sophie Slezak. We also honor those Sisters celebrating 50 years of ministry: Sisters Margaret McCleary and Priscilla St. Pierre. As we honor these jubilarians, we give thanks to God for the 460 years of service these women have given to our Church.

The women we honor today responded long ago to a call from God and have lived a life of vowed service with consistency and conviction. They have lived and served in the pre-Vatican II and post-Vatican II Church. They have endured both eras with fidelity and have prevailed with distinction.

Today, I have the privilege of expressing the gratitude and affection of all who gather in this holy place. Today, I have the honor of praying with all of you that God's love will continue to sustain and enliven our jubilarians in their ministry.

Sisters, when you entered your community, you responded to the call of Abraham: "Come to the place to which I will show you." (Genesis 12:1) Like Abraham, you followed that call. My sincere prayer is that you continue to hear and follow that call in these golden and diamond years of ministry.

I am humbled to be your chaplain and honored to be your friend.

Know that God—and each of us, your grateful guests—love you for who you are and all the good you do.

Father Hugh F. Crean
(1937–2015)

Illustration by Jim Trelease

Father Hugh F. Crean was ordained to the priesthood following four years of study at Saint Mary's Seminary, located in Baltimore, Maryland. This photo was used in media releases announcing his ordination.

"Wisdom means many things. It means carefully observing the world around us, recognizing the things that really matter."

—Father Hugh F. Crean

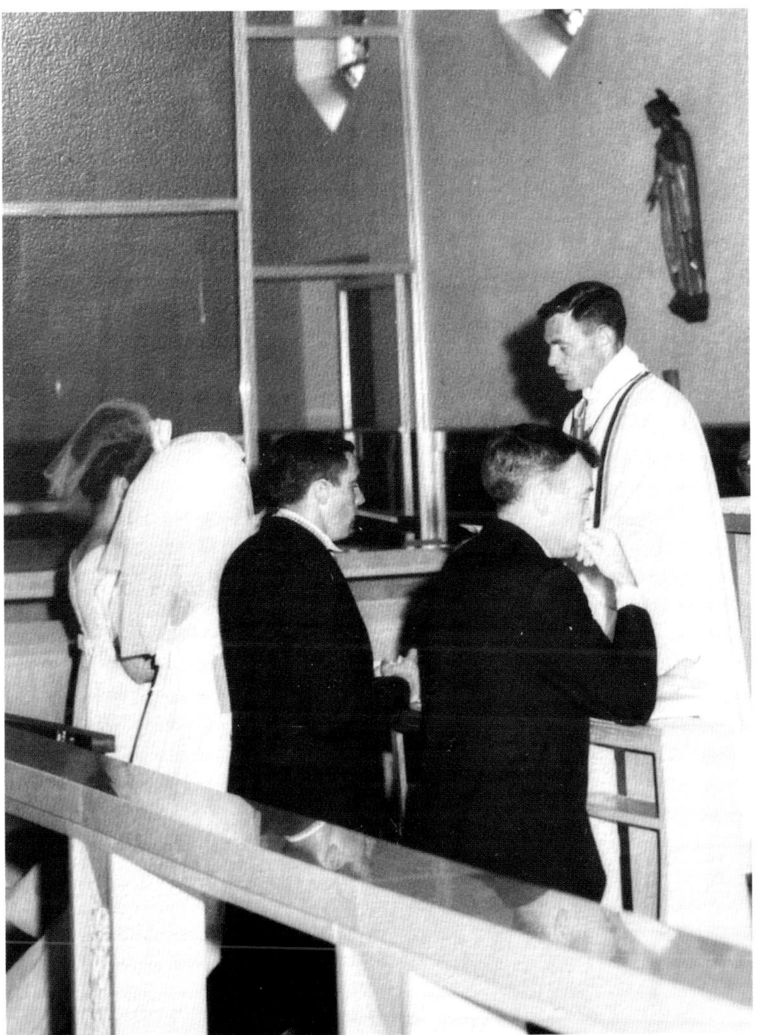

Hugh officiating at the wedding of his brother Bill to Joan Dickinson in 1968. The ceremony took place in Saint Paul's Church in Springfield, Massachusetts.

During his four years in Louvain, Hugh had the opportunity to travel throughout much of Europe during semester breaks. This photo was taken in 1971 during a ski trip in the Alps.

Hugh was assigned to the University of Louvain for doctoral studies between 1969 and 1973.
This photo was taken in 1972 as Hugh studied for comprehensive exams.

Following doctoral studies in Louvain, Hugh was assigned to Elms College in Chicopee, Massachusetts, where he taught theology for seven years. This photo appeared in the 1978 *Elmata*, the college's yearbook.

"God loves people of humility, faith, and trust. God is here with open arms of embrace to all of you. Believe and trust. With God, walk the journey to the place He will show you along the way."

—Father Hugh F. Crean

In this 1982 photo, Hugh is joined by Father Howard McCormick (far left) and Father George Farland at Mont Marie in Holyoke, Massachusetts, the motherhouse of the Sisters of St. Joseph of Springfield, for a final profession ceremony.

Hugh with Bishop Joseph Maguire (center) and Father George Farland in 1984 on the steps of City Hall in Springfield. That year, Hugh and George received the Burke Award, which is presented by the Springfield Saint Patrick's Day Committee in memory of John and Agnes Burke. The award honors individuals who have made important contributions to the Irish community in Springfield.

The son of immigrants, Hugh took deep pride in his Irish roots. Here, Hugh and his only sister, Sheila, visit Ireland in 1984.

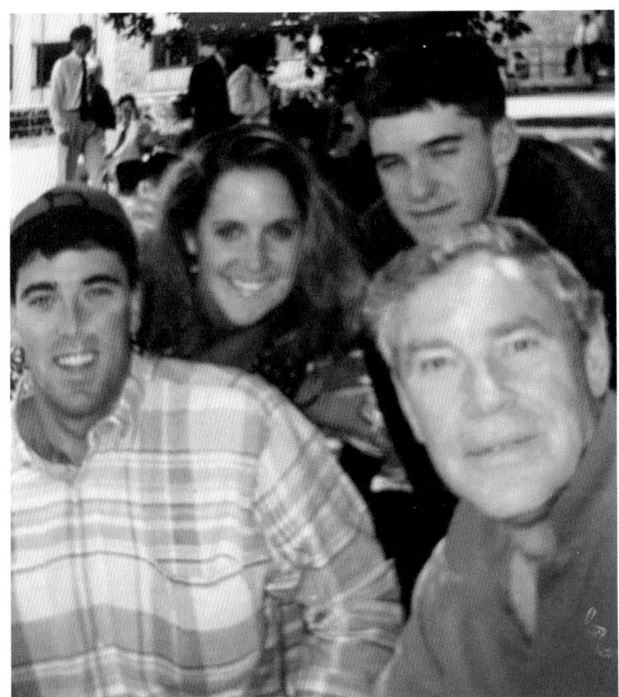

Hugh vacationed over the years in Westerly, Rhode Island. Family and friends visited him often. Seen in this 2001 photo are Hugh's niece Kelly and nephews Billy and Kevin.

This photo was taken with members of Hugh's immediate family in 2002, during one of their many visits to Hugh's vacation home in Westerly.

Hugh with nephew Jerry Crean, his wife, Beth Crean, and their son Shay Crean immediately following Shay's baptism in 2005.

"Throughout my life, I cared more about relationships than possessions. I love all of you and want you to love and look out for each other. Your love for one another will prove itself to be the most important gift in life."

—Father Hugh F. Crean

Hugh was recognized as a gifted homilist. In this 2010 photo taken in Sacred Heart Church in Springfield, Hugh delivers a homily in conjunction with the annual Saint Francis Xavier Novena.

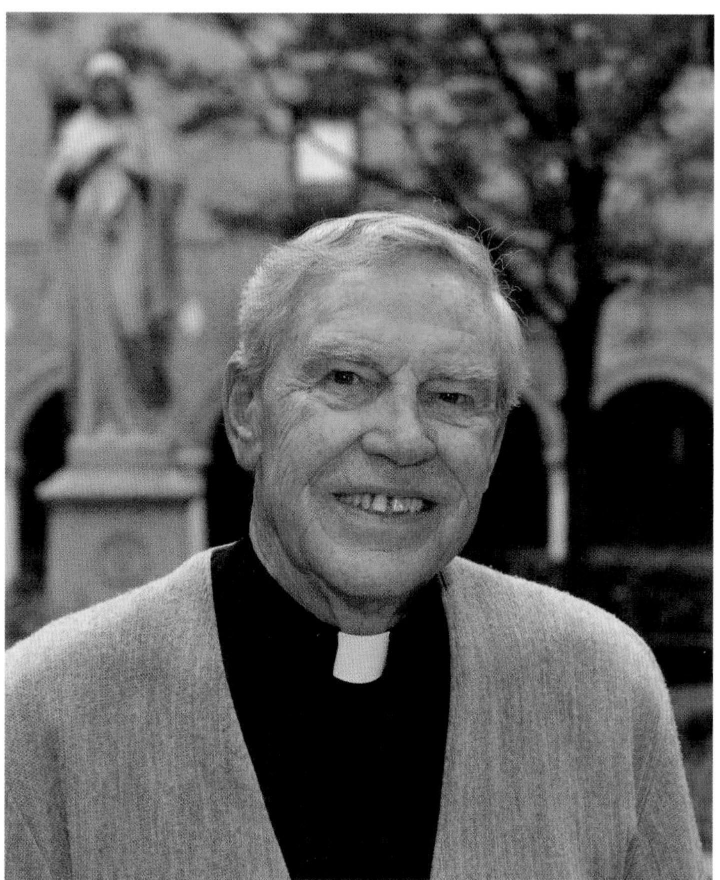

In this 2011 photo, Hugh is seen near the entryway of Providence Place in Holyoke, Massachusetts.

Hugh preaching during a Mass celebrated on June 24, 2012, in Our Lady of the Blessed Sacrament Church in Westfield, Massachusetts, on the occasion of his fiftieth anniversary of ordination.

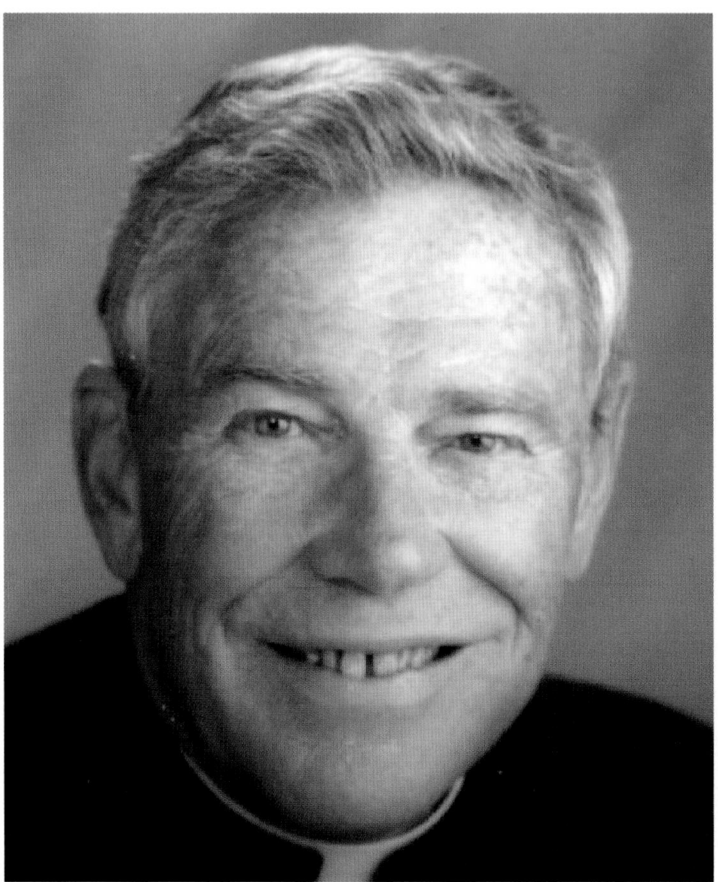

This 2012 photo was used in media coverage of Hugh's fiftieth anniversary of ordination to the priesthood.

Members of Hugh's family gather following a Mass in 2012 celebrating his fiftieth anniversary of ordination to the priesthood. This celebration took place in Our Lady of the Blessed Sacrament Church and Parish Center, both located in Westfield.

Hampden County Sheriff and good friend Michael Ashe congratulates Hugh in 2012 on the occasion of Hugh's fiftieth anniversary celebration.

Hugh's retirement apartment at Providence Place in Holyoke, 2012.

Hugh's grandnephew Charlie and sister, Sheila, are seen visiting Providence Place in Holyoke in 2013.

Christmas Letter to the Andrews Family

Jim Andrews was Hugh's childhood friend. Hugh used retirement from active ministry as an occasion to write letters to friends and family. In this 2007 letter, Hugh shares memories and expresses gratitude.

THIS IS NOT an easy letter for me to write. Nonetheless, I want to tell you about your father, who died at the young age of 43. I want to tell you how I knew him. It is the only Christmas present I can give you.

Jim Andrews was my friend from our first year in high school. We were simple, impressionable young men who were "sneaking up on the mystery of adulthood."

He was bright, intelligent, engaging, witty, playful, popular, and active in everything. Saint Mary's Parish High School was fun. He was a "brown nose" and the Sisters loved him! (I must admit that your dad thought I was a "brown nose" too!)

Saint Mary's was a small school where we received a great education. We were involved in all kinds of activities from sports to French and Latin Clubs. Weekly exams, trips with the debating team to other schools, and cherished friendships were part of life at Saint Mary's.

After high school, I went to Holy Cross College. Your father entered Saint Charles College Seminary. We saw each other infrequently, but remained steadfast friends through those four years, 1954–1958.

In 1958, I graduated from Holy Cross College and entered Saint Mary's Seminary in Baltimore as a classmate of your father. He left the seminary in 1960, began a new and flourishing career, and met your mother. The rest is history!

I loved your father. We were more like brothers than friends. I miss him every day. He succeeded in life as a businessman, publisher, husband, father, and exceptionally good person.

Unfortunately, your father died too young. He left behind a heritage of integrity, honor, and wisdom. He left behind a wonderful wife, two fine sons with great wives, and grandchildren he would cherish.

This Christmas, I wanted to rekindle for myself and for you the flame of memory, not so much to mourn, but to venerate the life and goodness of a very fine person, husband, father, friend, and visionary, James Frederick Andrews. Jim Andrews, who is gone but not forgotten.

Please know of my support and affection for all of you as your families grow and your careers unfold under the watchful vigilance of your father.

I am with you in any and every way as you raise your families and engage the world with the spirit, wisdom, and goodness gleaned from your father and my dearest friend.

With my love, prayers, and care always,
Father Hugh

Last Will and Testament

This is one of the last meditative reflections written by Hugh.

MY LAST WILL and testament reflects my love for my family.

Most of my nephews and nieces seem to be managing their lives very well. In the spirit of our family tradition and values, I ask them to "look out" for each other spiritually, emotionally, financially, and socially. Sheila, Jack, Bill, and I learned an enormous amount about life from the faith and integrity of our parents who never had more than six years of formal education in Ireland.

I never knew my grandparents, but I had gifted, caring, hardworking, fun, and loving parents named Hugh and Nora (Brosnan) Crean. For them, goodness was far more important than possessions, virtue mattered more than money, family pride revered more than appearance. These attributes were shared by Nora and Hugh with Sheila, John, Hugh, and William. Did we adequately acknowledge and incorporate these virtues into our lives? Only God knows.

John died young. He was a businessman who had a lust for life his frail body could not contain. He wanted to be many things at the same time: a mystic, philosopher, merchant, and father. His time with us was too short. Nonetheless, he left behind a legacy of six children still seeking the key to life as he did when he died at the age of 33. He loved his children, although he only knew them as toddlers.

Bill also died young. He was the most idealistic man I ever knew. Goodness defined his being and his doing. He was kind, gracious, strong, brave, manly, and competent. He was loved by everyone. Everyone respected and admired Bill. People loved Bill more than he loved himself.

Sheila was the eldest. She was the darling of my mother and confidante of my mother. Sheila had three lives. As a young girl, she was nurtured in our family home. She was a Sister of St. Joseph for 22 years and served as a teacher and religious superior. At the age of 41, she began the third phase of her life. Seven years later, she married Bob Rheault, a widower. Bob and Sheila lived happily until he died in 1994. Sheila is the treasure of our family. She is a mystic. She is a caring friend.

I love my nieces and nephews equally. Throughout my life, I cared more about relationships than possessions. I love all of you and want you to love and look out for each other. Your love for one another will prove itself to be the most important gift in life.

Hugh, Ann, Norine, Mark, John, Michael, Jennifer, Bill, Kelly, Hugh, Gerald, and Kevin: May God give you the grace and wisdom to do the right thing at the right time and for the right reason.

Thank you for being my family.

Thank you for being "my" children and my joy.

With all my love,
Uncle Hugh

Part Two

The Creans, Westfield, and Saint Mary's Parish

JANE F. MORRISEY, SSJ, PHD

WHEN I OPEN my eyes to Hugh Crean's childhood neighborhood, his parish, and school, I become the child I still am and follow him. I know that I'll not catch up with him—he arrived four years before me. Eighty years now have passed since I was born and began life near Hugh's family. These years later, I am yet witness. The landscape is familiar, and, now that his life has moved past death, I have his words to follow, to recognize, to honor. They let me see as he saw and recounted. I do lag behind, but in my mind and ink, I tell those times of his life as he wrote them down at various intervals.

As for each of us, "in the beginning" was his family. In his "Last Will and Testament," Hugh tells it this way: "I never knew my grandparents, but I had gifted, caring, proud, religious, hardworking parents—Hugh and Nora (Brosnan) Crean. For them, goodness was more important than possessions, virtue valued more than money, family pride more than appearance. . . . Did we (their children) acknowledge and incorporate (these attributes) into our lives?" Hugh answers his own question in three true words: "Only God knows!" In his life and verbal legacy, he does, however, give us real insights into what he thinks and why.

In April 2007, at age seventy, Hugh began to sketch a three-page memoir of his early life as the third child in a family with four children. His impressions float between his parents' chiaroscuro recollections of their relatives in Ireland as he experienced them day-to-day at their home in Westfield, Massachusetts. "My family in our early days knew only our parents' memories of Ireland. I vividly remember my father's grief and my mother's tears when they received the infrequent sad news of parents and relatives who died in Ireland. I wept for my mother, who was tender, soft, silent, and strong—I mourned for my father, who caressed us and carried on."

As a child, I knew Hugh's father as the one who in the morning opened and closed the doors in my home around the corner from theirs at 19 Belmont Street. I can hear the door and the footsteps, remember the clink of ice, and imagine the heft of oil delivered outside the kitchen in my family's Franklin Street apartment. I learned from his obituary that he later worked at Stevens Paper Mills. At eighteen years old, Mr. Crean departed from Castlegregory in rural Ireland and joined his sisters Catherine Crean and Hannah Crean Shea and his brother Patrick in the rapidly developing city of Westfield. He was thirty when he married Nora Brosnan. She was twenty-seven. She had come to Westfield because her Uncle Dennis was there. Her only sister to join her "stateside" died in her early thirties in neighboring Springfield.

Young Hugh nobly bore his father's name and was sensitive to his parents' past and present. The elder Hugh and his wife were born into Kerry families, each with six children. A growing number of family members of their generation would live their early lives as a clan of family and neighbors. No one would live alone. When cousins migrated from Ireland to follow in their footsteps, Hugh and Nora opened their doors to their siblings' children. When a parent died, the children had a home in their home. John J. and Joseph P. Daly and Rosemary Pniak are listed as Mr. Crean's children in his 1969 obituary. When his namesake gave his mother Nora's eulogy twenty-one years later, he added the names of Gerry Murphy, Margaret Brosnan, Eileen and Mary Crean, and Mary Sullivan to the litany of those who claimed home and family at 19 Belmont.

All their lives, the Crean family members opened their hearts and doors to unifying love. Hugh captured the spirit and substance of this when he served as marshal for the Sons of Erin's Saint Patrick's Day Parade. He said, "The spirit of Ireland is the blood in my veins—the joy of my life and the pride of my heritage." He knew where he had learned not to leave anyone behind.

In that same address, Hugh began to describe his family's city as home, saying, "I was born, nurtured, educated, and sneaked up on the mystery of adulthood in Westfield." Elsewhere, he detailed the freedom, burden, and joy of "sneaking up" on that mystery in his immigrant family's New World. He asked simply, "What did we know?"

He immediately summarized family life as a cycle of children's activity and understanding: "little kids playing ball, enjoying life, growing up happy with loving parents who spoke differently from the other parents but also loved us with ardent affection—not only for Sheila (their darling), Jack (their first-born son), but (also) Hugh and William (named after my mother's doctor, who carried her through a very difficult delivery)." (I, too, fondly remember our city's Doctor Connery and can envision the office where he gently tended to "all his children's" scrapes and scratchy breathing.)

Family was bloodline and community, both intact and inclusive. For the Creans, family meant home, neighborhood, parish, school, and city. At age fourteen, Hugh felt in a singular way his father's loss when Sheila, the eldest child, left home to become a Sister of St. Joseph. He wrote how his father missed his sister, but nonetheless "visits to Mont Marie (the Sisters' Mother House in Holyoke) were tender, loving, and caressing experiences for us—but she was gone." One can see his adolescent smile in the words that follow: "I got her bed and room!" Until Sheila left home, he'd shared his bed with Billy.

Young Hugh lived life fully "near the dike, played ball on the playgrounds and the city gymnasiums, worked the tobacco fields, studied at Saint Mary's schools, and danced at the Friday night hops." For our families, "The Dike" was the site of Fourth of July fireworks and the summer stomping ground of the Ringling Bros. and Barnum & Bailey Circus. I'm told that Hugh and his friends would frequently go swimming at the dike but knew to wait until a neighbor, returning home from the mills, would dive in to wash his sweat away. The boys would jump in after their "lifeguard's" arrival. I can smell the pungent aroma of miles and miles of tobacco fields stretching through the Pioneer Valley. I can hear the strains of bagpipes lifting feet high after winter's piles of snow and accompanying local and regional Saint Patrick's Day parades, celebrations, and funerals. The hops were an integral part of the Church and city's social life since 1939. I can see Mr. Fred Degregorio chaperoning at Saint Mary's every week and one of the priests circling the basement dance floor like a village matchmaker, kindly alert to wallflowers.

Saint Mary's Parish and School nurtured us in full family life. These were the buildings in which we prayed together, studied together, became who we are together—Irish or not. Joyce, the firstborn in my family, was a classmate of Billy, the youngest of Hugh and Nora's children. I was a year behind her. I looked up to the Crean children. At school and in church, our circle of family grew to include friends and faculty and those generous neighbors, staff, and volunteers who coached the teams, led the choir, directed the plays and minstrel shows, and prepared students for the sacraments.

At Saint Mary's, faith grew, fostering friendship and building community. The parish buildings weren't far from the Sons of Erin or the converging rivers that created the dike. The railway had come to town and was replacing the canals. Through the 1940s and '50s, both parish and school grew under the leadership of the Father Patrick Dowd, Monsignor George Shea, and Sister Mary Thomasine (Anna Moriarty), SSJ.

The Sisters of St. Joseph of Springfield staffed the three-story elementary and high school. The years the Crean family attended Saint Mary's were the years Sister Thomasine, a true "giant," led the Way. She was the eighth of the eleven children in her family. Our congregation's first school, Saint Patrick's in Chicopee Falls, had been founded in 1883 across the street from her home. She was then thirteen years old. From the time of her entrance ten years later, she was actively engaged in teaching in the first schools the congregation established from western Massachusetts to Newport, Rhode Island.

She arrived at Saint Mary's in 1930 as Superior of the Convent and Principal of the School. Sister Thomasine was prepared for her task by undergraduate studies at Fordham University and graduate studies at Boston College, supplemented by one summer at McGill University in Canada. She knew what she was about, and so did Saint Mary's students. She headed the grammar and high schools for thirty years. She left no doubt in anyone's mind that "excellence" was education's end, and whether faculty member, student, priest, or parent, everyone learned that, within school walls, she was "in charge." My brother Richard recently told me that he thought through his school years that Thomasine was the synonym of "principal." An early parish history reports: "The school grew, and in the late 1940s classrooms were full; but even at eighty and some years, she kept stern watch over a school in which she boasted there wasn't an incorrigible child. Generations of children had passed under her discerning eye." She paid her last visit to students at age ninety.

At Saint Mary's, Sheila, Jack, Hugh, and Billy Crean and their other family members and friends starred in sports, drama, debates, leadership, and faith, as had their parents and grandparents before them. You couldn't miss the Creans. They seemed to do everything and do it well. The Sisters and priests engaged with everyone in the school and all its activities. Hugh remembered fondly how the pastor came dressed like Santa every year to deliver a box of hard Christmas candy to each child.

Moreover, we learned that to live was to serve. Hugh's lifelong friends from those years, Jim Andrews and John (Okie) O'Connor, had stories to tell. Okie, still active at age eighty-five, recalled Ed Courtney, who, from his wheelchair, coached their championship Bi-County League basketball teams. Ed lived in a small house at the edge of the schoolyard. Hugh and Okie visited and wheeled him wherever he needed to be so he didn't miss practice or a game.

In the 1952 *Memento,* the school yearbook, the frontispiece acclaims the schoolhouse as the place:

> . . . where we "grew in wisdom, grace and age"
> with Christ, the model of youth,
> in Whose Image we learned to PRAY TOGETHER;
> under Whose Guidance we learned to WORK TOGETHER;
> motivated by Whose Love, we learned to PLAY TOGETHER.

A random sample of qualities and activities listed in Hugh's senior yearbook indicate that he learned and led as he was taught:

> Class president 3, 4;
> Dramatics 2, 3, 4;
> Basketball and baseball 1, 2, 3, 4;
> Dance Committee 1, 2, 3, 4;
> Debates 3, 4;
> Schola Virgilii President 4;
> Boys' State Representative 3.
>
> He is "Hughie" . . . handsome . . . popular . . .
> sterling character . . . friend to all . . .
> terrific on the court . . . has many secret admirers . . .
> a dandy dancer . . . a smooth dresser.

Although Hugh's siblings' dreams and aspirations would later be abbreviated by death at an early age or skewed and scarred by the inevitable suffering of human limitations, ill health, or the toll of poverty, war, and violence, their legacy embodies the mission of their childhood educators, the Sisters of St. Joseph of Springfield. Since the Congregation's founding in France in 1650, it has aimed to be a "Congregation of God's Great Love." Its mission derives from Jesus' prayer the night before he died, "That all may be One."

In many ways, Hugh faithfully and publicly acknowledged his indebtedness to his childhood teachers. At some point before he died, he listed on a piece of lined paper his "Memorable Teachers" from grade school through doctoral studies at the Louvain in Belgium. They number twelve, and half of them are from Saint Mary's School:

> Sister Helen Elizabeth, Grade 2,
> Sister Mary Christopher, Grade 3,
> Sister Vincent Clare, Grade 8,
> Sister Mary Fidelis, Grade 9,
> Sister Andrew Maria, Grade 11,
> Sister Marita Joseph, Grade 12

On two occasions, Hugh wrote a "Reflection on Wisdom." Each reflection gives a sense of what really mattered to him in all he had learned from the beginning. In the more recent version, delivered at a Jubilee Celebration of the Sisters of St. Joseph of Springfield, he champions the legacy from his childhood. It reflects the Word of the Gospel made flesh. He wrote:

> Wisdom means many things.
> It means carefully observing the world around us, recognizing the things that really matter.
> It means reflecting on the lilies of the field, the birds of the air, and learning timeless lessons from them.
> It means observing old and young people who are signs of unselfishness and generosity for us to imitate.
> It means not making judgements rashly.
> It means giving and receiving forgiveness and offering people a second chance.
> It means listening when we are tempted to speak.

> It means finding the right words to speak at the right time, and for the right reason.
> It means balance, tolerance, optimism, and hope.

His words of and on wisdom encapsulate the way he lived in and beyond this world through eyes of love. He experienced disappointment and loss—who doesn't?—but had met the vagaries of life with understanding, acceptance, and unfailing love. When Sheila left the Sisters of St. Joseph in the '70s to live, in his words, as "a secular mystic" and, later, as caretaker for her mother and as a wife, stepmother, widow, and finally a patient for years at the Sisters' Health Care Center on the very site where she had entered the congregation, he embraced her choices and understood. When his brother Jack, brilliant businessman, entrepreneur, and father of five with a sixth child in the womb, died at age thirty-three and his widow later remarried Hugh's high school classmate and friend, he accepted and loved them all. When his younger brother Billy died of cancer in his early fifties, leaving his wife and children, he accepted all who would follow for the rest of his life.

In his words and deeds, his family eulogies, and public addresses, we can see from his childhood that when life was tested by fire, Hugh Crean learned to love deeply. In his 1992 eulogy for his second-grade teacher, Sister Helen Elizabeth, SSJ, he so described her part in his education. "Helen," he said, "you taught so many of us . . . to live with intensity; to rejoice in adversity; to prevail with tenacity. You taught us to love with reckless abandon." Ten years prior to that prayer at her casket, he had invited young student leaders in the Cathedral High National Honor Society to "care a little more and love a little more because of all you have learned of Christ." He quoted Pierre Teilhard de Chardin: "Someday after mastering the winds and waves, the tides and gravity, we shall harness for God the energies of love. And then, for the second time in the history of our world, the human race will have discovered fire."

Reflections on American Catholic History

DAVID J. O'BRIEN, PHD

> My Lord God, I have no idea where I am going. I do not see the road ahead of me. I cannot know for certain where it will end. Nor do I really know myself, and the fact that I think that I am following your will does not mean that I am actually doing so. But I believe that the desire to please you does in fact please you. And I hope I have that desire in all that I am doing. I hope that I will never do anything apart from that desire. And I know that if I do this you will lead me by the right road, though I may know nothing about it. Therefore will I trust you always, though I may seem to be lost and in the shadow of death. I will not fear, for you are ever with me, and you will never leave me to face my perils alone.
>
> —Thomas Merton, *Thoughts in Solitude*

I WAS HONORED to offer the annual Father Hugh Crean Lecture at the College of Our Lady of the Elms in 2021, and I am very grateful to have it included in this book dedicated to the memory of Father Crean. When President Dumay invited me to offer the lecture, he pointed out that our Catholic Church had dedicated 2021 to Saint Joseph. So, I tried to offer some thoughts about our American Catholic history—past, present, and future—informed at least a little by reflection on Saint Joseph, a reflection assisted by Pope Francis's quite remarkable apostolic letter[1] announcing the year. Pope Francis bows to tradition with mention of Pope Pius IX's naming Saint Joseph patron of the universal Church. Then he acknowledges his own long-standing devotion to Saint Joseph as protective father of the Holy Family and as patron of workers. And Pope Francis also refers to the flight into and unknown stay in Egypt, linking Saint Joseph to today's families of refugees and asylum seekers.

More broadly, Pope Francis refers to Saint Joseph's remarkably steadfast faith and trust when everything in his world turned upside down. His beloved

1 "Patris Corde," issued on December 8, 2020.

bride-to-be became pregnant by the Holy Spirit. The child, he was told, would fulfill God's promises to his people, Israel, but was then targeted for death by the civil authorities. Born in circumstances far from the centers of power, Joseph knew from these experiences that his son, Jesus, would always make religious authorities uneasy. There was danger everywhere, institutions were destabilized, taken-for-granted expectations of all the Jewish parties were being shattered, and the future must have seemed scary, except for Joseph's faith and trust in God. Amid this near total displacement, Joseph shows what Pope Francis calls "creative courage," responding to God's invitation in dreams and life circumstances in a spirit the Pope says would later be called "Christian realism."

If Joseph's decision to stand with Mary suggests our need to trust the ones we love, and his family's flight to Egypt suggests making a place in our hearts and homelands for people in flight from oppression, recalling earlier migrants such as my grandparents and many of yours, then perhaps his experience of crumbling political and religious establishments and disappointed community expectations suggests our context for this lecture honoring Hugh Crean, a leader and lover of the Church of Springfield. Pope Francis suggests we should follow in the way of Saint Joseph's faith-filled realism, trusting God and one another and looking for God's invitation in our prayer, in our Christian movement, in our encounters with others, especially the poor, and in the ever-moving providential story of God's family, which of course means everybody, everywhere.

Thinking about our experience, those of us who were, like Hugh Crean, Vatican II-era priests, religious, and laypersons, we might find some connections with Saint Joseph's experience of the disruption of his settled Jewish life. In that spirit, I offer some thoughts on the recent history of American Catholicism.

Hugh Crean and I were born and raised in the Golden Age of American Catholicism. He graduated from Holy Cross in 1958. I came from Pittsfield and was slated for Holy Cross, but instead I went to Notre Dame, graduating in 1960. That year one of our own, John Kennedy, was running for president. President Eisenhower was our commencement speaker; the baccalaureate Mass was celebrated by Cardinal Montini of Milan, who a few years later became Pope (now Saint) Paul VI; and our hearts were with the critically ill honorary degree recipient, Dr. Tom Dooley, whose medical service in Indochina earned him the title Doctor America. Over the door of Notre Dame Basilica are the words

"God, Country, Notre Dame." They fit together, and we loved all three, our own Holy Trinity.

Since then, few if any of us have had messages from angels, as Saint Joseph did, but like him we have experienced what philosopher Charles Taylor[2] calls the "unbundling" of our once integrated religious and national faith. In 1960, I set out to study American political history as a possible way of making a contribution to the American history being made around me. God turned my haphazard career choice into a vocation in ways I had not expected. I took a room with a couple who turned out to be Catholic Workers, and they drew me to Catholic ideas I had not encountered at Notre Dame and to our own American Catholic history. The University of Rochester, a generous foundation and later patient college employers, actually paid me to study American Catholic history while observing and, with my Joanne occasionally joining projects for Catholic and American renewal and reform, meeting Hugh Crean along the way.

Like other Vatican II-era Catholics, we had a few tastes of Saint Joseph's disrupting experience in the decade after I left Notre Dame. There was racism I had little noticed earlier, and then came wars, which I had always supported, and assassinations of heroes I had come to admire. These public events and personal encounters shook taken-for-granted institutions and what had earlier seemed self-evident ideas. There were liberating moments—many of them, to be sure—but also emerging divisions and explosions of senseless violence. Idealistic friends joined the Peace Corps, and we sent other young men, some equally idealistic, abroad to kill and too often die for us. But, like Saint Joseph, many of us had the sense that while all this disruption was happening—seen with at least a little of Pope Francis's Christian realism—something new was being born. There was creative courage, to use that other Pope Francis phrase, in the historic decisions made at the Vatican Council, in the words and witness of Dorothy Day[3] and her friends across the country, in the suggestive contemplation and commentaries of Thomas Merton[4] in his hermitage, in the witness of Philip and Daniel Berrigan,[5]

---

2 Canadian philosopher, b. 1931.

3 American journalist and activist (1897–1980).

4 American Trappist monk, writer, and theologian (1915–1968).

5 American priests and peace activists (1923–2002 and 1921–2016).

led smiling to jail, in Cesar Chavez[6] and Dolores Huerta[7] in California vineyards and fields, and in the Sisters of St. Joseph's exploring new ways of living the joy of the Gospel right around here.

Vatican II priests such as Hugh Crean, my own mentor and friend Monsignor John Egan of Chicago, and so many others helped us find hope in the Council, the civil rights movement, the Christian peace movement, and the amazing work across the world of our Church, newly committed, it seemed, to human rights, peacemaking, and social justice. Catholicism and Americanism no longer quite fit together, but we thought we could join movements to help fix both and bring them closer together in work for a better world. I am confident that Hugh Crean and his Springfield-area friends shared that excitement about Catholic renewal and reform. He dug deeply into the challenge of renewal in his doctoral work, exploring the way faith and doubt were not opponents but companions as we encounter our God in the "signs" of our particular and troubled times. As with so many priests of his generation, Hugh committed himself to pastoral ministry with his people, sharing that responsibility with bishops, brother priests, deacons, and religious women.

But things did not work out quite as we expected. I noted my discovery of new resources of Catholic thought and imagination when I left Notre Dame in 1960. Now I take note of another personal anniversary. Fifty years ago, in 1970–71, ten years after I met those Catholic Workers in Rochester, New York, some good Protestant philanthropists awarded me a fellowship to take a year off from my brand-new job at Holy Cross to study theology at Harvard Divinity School and the Jesuit's Weston School of Theology. During that year, I thought about what was going on in my community of American Catholics, in our civil religion as well as our Church, during the ten years since I had graduated from Notre Dame. In a book I wrote that year, *The Renewal of American Catholicism,* and in many talks later, I tried to help our communities understand the shared history we were experiencing—and the history we were making—during those ten years, years even a mild-mannered historian such as my friend Philip Gleason[8] spoke of as the disintegration of American Catholicism as we had known it.

---

6 American labor leader and civil rights activist (1927–1993).

7 American labor leader and civil rights activist, b. 1930.

8 American history educator at the University of Notre Dame, b. 1927.

My central idea was that we were living through the end of the remarkably successful subculture American Catholics had constructed over two centuries. The decade was intense because three intersecting explosions made it seem as if everything was changing, all at once.

First of all, we were changing. Our families and communities had constructed parishes and schools, social services agencies and hospitals, trade unions and political machines, all while holding fast to their religious heritage. As one historian put it, "folk memories brought to bear on new aspirations"[9] enabled the formation of immigrant, working-class communities and, in turn, led my aunt to the Sisters of St. Joseph, my uncle with Maryknoll to Korea, Hugh Crean to Louvain, and Dave O'Brien to Notre Dame. Now our immigrant, working-class, Euro-American Catholic families were moving up, out, and into: up social and economic ladders, out of tight urban parishes and neighborhoods, into automobile suburbs, professional practices, management jobs, and even boardrooms. I saw the process as Americanization, its spirit fueled by our own versions of Americanism, ideas that made that movement up, out, and into not only okay but providential, allowing us at last to take a full share of responsibility for our Church and our country.

While all this was happening, so did Vatican II. Our Church finally caught up with us by affirming religious liberty and the separation of Church and state. Boundaries between Catholics and Protestants, between Christians and Jews, between "the men and women of this age" and "the followers of Christ" all became permeable. Mass was now celebrated in our own languages; altars were turned around; we were told the people of God came first, before clergy and hierarchy; and on the issue of most interest to my generation—birth control—we made much of new references to conscience. Almost everybody welcomed these changes, and the journals I read seemed to say that, like us, the Church was becoming more and more American. Theologian Karl Rahner[10] said that, in the future, faith would become "a matter of personal decision, constantly renewed, amid perilous surroundings." That seemed okay to us, although another theologian, John Courtney Murray,[11] worried

9 Timothy L. Smith, historian and educator (1924–1997).

10 German priest and theologian (1904–1984).

11 American priest and theologian (1904–1967).

about what might happen when Catholics began to explore their religious freedom and formation of conscience in their own relations with the Church and the state.

And while all this was going on, it was "the '60s," and I was not alone in learning more than I had expected about race and class and gender, about the dark sides of my civil religion. In 1965, as the Council closed, it waffled a bit on conscience and birth control, but, while reaffirming just war teaching, the Council Fathers said for the first time that a Catholic could refuse military service. At that very moment, in early 1965, President Johnson sent our troops into conflict in Vietnam. Before long, there would be a half million men in that fight. The American Church had long supported the government of South Vietnam, but, now, as troubling questions arose and just war teaching suggested caution, prominent leaders spoke of Christian nonviolence, and in Worcester the bishop joined Protestant and Jewish leaders to launch an interfaith draft counseling center. The '60s, with all that happened, was the same period in which Vatican II's unexpected reforms were taking place, or, as with birth control, not taking place, and we ourselves were changing, agents of our own history. And we had the help of priests such as Hugh Crean, who loved the Church and shared our hope that a bold new era of creative, engaged Catholicism in our communities would enrich our Church and help change the world.

It is now fifty years since I paused to read some theology and write that book. A lot has happened in those fifty years. Once again we, the American Catholic people, have changed, the legacy of Vatican II is contested, and many of the struggles of the '60s are still with us. I don't have to tell people in Massachusetts about the impact of sin within our Church, and all of us are anxious about our country's political divisions and the huge challenges facing all of us. Far more than fifty years ago, everything now seems up for grabs, folk memories seem a bit thinner and more complicated, and many of us hunger for new aspirations for our own lives, and for our country and our Church.

We get some help in finding some of that "creative courage" of Saint Joseph celebrated by Pope Francis from the Canadian Catholic philosopher Charles Taylor. His provocative assessment of our situation suggests that my rather optimistic reading of the decade of the '60s fifty years ago hinted at a lingering American innocence. Today, it seems clear that the changes I noted were part of a wider transformation of Western culture that we are still trying to figure out. Taylor is very critical of our usual ideas of secularism, a term easily weaponized in culture wars. How often we blame society for our problems, as if society is not ours. Instead of secularization, he uses the term "unbundling" to describe the way in which areas of life—family and community, education and social services, private and public morality—were once integrated around faith and often under the influence and direct or indirect control of the Church (think of his Quebec or my ancestral Ireland) but became detached from one another. For the Catholic Church, the process was twofold:

1) The decline, marginalization, and eventual end of integrated Christian societies: Christendom as a memory, fueling passions for restoration for one faction of Church and society. This was often associated before World War II with a poisonous nationalism in Europe. Here in the United States, as I indicated, we were a minority, with no claim to take over, but our subculture retained many of the assumptions of Christendom. As the lay theologian Frank Sheed[12] put it years ago: "We are the sweet, selected few/the rest of you are damned/there isn't room enough for you/we can't have heaven crammed." We have a taste of those lingering resistance passions in America's Christian nationalists, and similar feelings inform some wider negative reaction to growing diversity and to perceptions of state or market pressures against what now seem to be traditional ideals and practices.

For some Catholics, here and elsewhere, what is hard to accept is that religion has become, as Rahner said before the Council, "a matter of personal decision constantly renewed amid perilous surroundings." That reality of individualism/personalism is accompanied by another: the multiplication of options in what resembles a religious marketplace. That combination of freedom of conscience and religious pluralism upsets many strong Catholic impulses; it also helps explain Pope Francis's emphasis on attraction more than persuasion, encounter rather than exclusion, dialogue rather than proclamations. It also helps explain many of our pastoral challenges everywhere from the family and the parish to Elms College.

2) Within the Church, there has been a similar "unbundling" of various facets of Catholic life. Where worship and prayer and education and social services

12 Australian-born lawyer, writer, and theologian (1897–1981).

were once carried on under one umbrella held by clergy and bishops over laity and religious, now those areas are often separated from one another, and there are options, plenty of them, within as well as outside the now very permeable boundaries of Catholicism. Think of our own bewildering associations every day, often requiring shifts in language and comportment—from family to workplace to book club to prayer group to extended family to political meeting. And our Church becomes more segmented with us. Within the Church, I was warned years ago about the separation of pastoral and social ministry, for which we have paid a great price. In higher education, the Vatican and bishops have repeatedly complained about a supposed loss of Catholic identity, while many of us worried about disconnection from the other Catholic institutions and ministries. Massimo Faggioli[13] has highlighted the separation of academic theology from pastoral work and experience, and now we are faced with the cost of our inability to think together about the status of Catholic institutions receiving public support in medical care, social services, and higher education. Segmentation, fragmentation, conflicts, and resolutions ranging from passionate commitment to resigned indifference—all these are part of everyday experience, within as well as outside what we experience as Church.

After Vatican II, the American theologian John Courtney Murray, as I noted earlier, worried about what would happen when the religious liberty now affirmed by the Church began to inform the life of the Church itself. Scholars of American Protestant experience I met alerted me to Murray's concern. They showed that religious liberty led to religious diversity, and the combination of the two led to personalism and evangelical forms of piety and ministry, attentiveness to scripture with a populist hermeneutic—the Bible as the people's book—calls to conversion and reconversion, revivalism, voluntary communities, congregationalism and affinity parishes, and a social and personal moral compass caught in the popular WWJD: "What would Jesus do?" For Protestants then and all-American Christians now, Church order sustained by unifying creeds and the authority of bishops and clergy, indeed Christian unity, intelligence, and moral discipline, in this world of diversity and freedom, were and are fragile at best, requiring deliberate attention and pastoral

13 Italian-born Church historian, educator, and writer, b. 1970.

creativity within an evangelical culture that is the default drive of democratic Christianity, certainly in America.

What all this means for us, Taylor suggests, is that we have entered what he calls "a new epoch." We have gained new freedom, and new responsibilities, in an emerging world where the old boundaries between sacred and secular, and between settled religious traditions, have become permeable at least. Some of us see huge benefits that speak of the Holy Spirit at work: people we know, indeed whole groups of people around us who used to accept their places and keep quiet, now walk with heads held high and eyes locked in on others, often with chips on their shoulders. A variety of spiritual and religious options affirm human dignity and nurture aspirations for personal authenticity, mutual respect, and some degree of justice and peace. Christianity always nurtured human dignity and sustained personal and family aspirations, as it did for so many of our families as they experienced economic, social, and political liberation. But that liberation also brought with it that unbundling; some things were lost, and freedom brought new and sometimes burdensome responsibilities, personal and public. And faith and Christian discipleship have indeed become matters of personal decision amid a perilous surrounding, a perilous surrounding that may now include the faith community itself. All religion, our religion, must now make its way through persuasion, not coercion, through attraction and authenticity more than power and control.

Robert Bellah,[14] the great sociologist who helped us recognize our civil religion, in later years said that America's was a basically Protestant culture. Our country was enriched, but sometimes crippled, by personalism, and he thought it badly needed the help of Catholic teachings and practices of solidarity. We Catholics, at about the same time, said that our Church and our community badly needed some of America's personalism, what Vatican II finally celebrated as "the dignity of the human person." In a way, both wishes came true, but not as we expected. America got a full dose of Catholicism in the Church's persistent support for immigrants, for economic justice, and for restraint in national security policy, but America also got organized participation by Catholics in the more sectarian sectors of the anti-abortion crusade and its anti-gay

14 American sociologist and educator (1927–2013).

and anti-feminist companions. Catholicism, for its part, got its full dose of American personalism in liberated women and men, in new forms of prayer and contemplative spirituality, and in voluntary efforts to reach out to people in need. But it also got individualism in its neoliberal clothing of limited government, low taxes, and deferral of moral issues to the market.

Charles Taylor thinks that we Christians should resist restorationist impulses, yearning for Christendom or more modest ethno-religious subcultures, and do our best to separate piety and power. But, at times, it appears that, instead, religious and moral differences have become highly politicized, and power has swallowed both of our old pieties, American and Christian. Why? Perhaps a clue lies in that earlier idea that our American Catholic subculture our forebears constructed arose from "folk memories" brought to bear on "new aspirations." What happens when future aspirations, when shared American dreams and Pope John XXIII's and Pope Francis's visions of global solidarity, fade into fantasy? If the future is treacherous and personal, family, and community hopes recede, then all we have are past and present. Perhaps then freedom from fear trumps freedom from want, history and memory become battlegrounds, and fewer of us search for a viable future.

For Hugh Crean and me, and for many others, that usable future was a story of past and present that drew us together, in freedom, to assist others to experience liberation from fear and want, and together build a better world. The key to our shared history may be the presence, or absence, of aspirations. For evidence of that possibility, we might pay attention to the last days and words of Martin Luther King Jr., as he saw his people, all of us, poised between "chaos and community." Dr. King, who always balanced human dignity and solidarity, changed hearts with his dream in 1963 and again on the night before he was murdered. That night, amid disruptions and disappointments Saint Joseph would have recognized, he reaffirmed his confidence that someday, somehow, we would reach that beloved kingdom at the center of his faith-filled imagination.

What of Pope Francis and other icons for us Americans like Thomas Merton and Dorothy Day? Here again Charles Taylor is a help.

In an informal talk, Taylor noted that among the consequences for the Catholic community of disruption, displacement, and ever-multiplying diversities is the popularity of the image of life as a journey. When life is viewed as a journey, one moves forward, learning about God's will and making what history one can. On this journey, the Christians among us try as best they can to build the Kingdom.

In many ways, Vatican II anticipated this image of life as a journey with its references to a "pilgrim church" that moves through many epochs and many cultures. As a pilgrim, the Church's encounters with people are characterized by tension given the Church's ambitious claims of being "the one true church, never in need of reform or development."

Taylor's informal talk also echoes a theme of Hugh Crean's doctoral work. In his dissertation, Hugh insists that as we experience our disrupted epoch, doubt becomes understood as a companion of a robust faith. In this regard, Taylor thinks the best image of the Church of the future is the mustard seed, planting seeds here and there. Some of these seeds are received with faith and provide nesting places for passing birds. Other seeds are received with doubt. Seeds received with doubt coexist with seeds received with faith.

In the midst of disruption, displacement, and ever-multiplying diversities in our world and Church, Merton shows us another way. Merton shows us the inner way. In solitude, Merton dove as deeply as anyone could into deep recesses of the Catholic intellectual and spiritual tradition. He eventually emerged from that sacred sanctuary not to rebuild Christendom but to seek God and wisdom everywhere, with everyone he met a potential companion on the journey. Merton emerged from the solitude, falling in love with the people he was once glad to leave behind. He's been dead since 1968, yet his words, wisdom, and solitude still move people and perhaps point one way to renewal of our Christian and American aspirations.

And then there's Dorothy Day, who is gone for forty years but perhaps is better known today than ever. Her journey had its inner path, to be sure, but her vocation was not Merton's plunge into solitude but into the world as it is, not as we would like it to be. Who better expressed the qualities of creative courage and faith-filled realism than Dorothy Day?

When I was young, people thought of Day as at the radical edge of the Church. In 1976, I was responsible for bringing her to a hearing held with two dozen American bishops. To my surprise, she was extremely nervous about facing bishops and being in front of television cameras. What she did not know was that the bishops on the panel were even more nervous about facing her. Dorothy Day was not worried about being on the radical edge of the Gospel. Her only worry was about finding the right way to challenge the bishops to care for the poor and work for peace.

When Dorothy Day died, I was asked to write a long obituary for *Commonweal* magazine. In part because of that experience, I wrote that she was not at the edge but at the center of our faith and our Church, living amid chaotic change, like Saint Joseph, doing God's will and trusting in God's ever-present love. Or, as Catholic Worker friends at the Mustard Seed Catholic Worker house in Worcester might say, scattering seeds; making space for whoever shows up; asking everyone to consider the possibilities of compassion and nonviolence; offering ideas about the common life, but even in the midst of small demonstrations and modest civil disobedience often displaying the same faithful and serene trust one finds in so many of our retired Sisters of St. Joseph. Like King and Merton, Dorothy Day expected, someday, to be with us all in the Kingdom of God. Pope Francis says that should generate "the joy of the Gospel." Dorothy found that joy sometimes in community and prayer and literature and sacraments. But disruptions not unknown to Saint Joseph sometimes made joy a bit distant, an aspiration; she called it "the duty of delight."

What might we who worry about our country and our Church be thinking about out of all this? Certainly, Hugh Crean, a genuine churchman, would ask us to keep thinking strategically about the important resources Catholicism can bring to American religion and American civil society. As one deeply committed to ecumenical dialogue, Hugh might suggest we relocate our thoughts about American Catholicism within the wider Christian movement, and that movement within interfaith dialogues and dialogues about civil religion, and with those who tell us they are not religious. As pastor, he might suggest we make a preferential but not exclusive option for the laity. How often our Catholic assessments and reflections are misdirected by near exclusive attention to what we are now once again calling the Church, and not meaning us. Instead, as with liberation theology, let's think about things in the first instance from the perspective of the laity and then determine to walk together, with our eyes on the prize, the

Kingdom of God, which, we are pretty sure, will most likely not be a great big Catholic Church.

As for the American side of our religious experience, certainly one lesson of our public history is that the American project of democratic self-government among people who disagree, sometimes over very serious matters, is profoundly endangered when its most liberated citizens no longer love it and acknowledge a full share of responsibility for its common life. In the 1890s, and again in the 1980s, Church leaders, and many theologians and scholars, deliberately rejected what they called Americanism and neo-Americanism. Nevertheless, it seems abundantly clear that the challenge that confronted pastorally oriented leaders from Isaac Hecker[15] to Hugh Crean was to provide a spirituality that would meet what Hecker called the "aspirations of nature" and answer "the questions of the soul" for honest and open seekers. For Hecker, it was among the ambitious, partially assimilated children of immigrants and the restless young Americans he met in idealistic communes and popular lecture halls. For Crean and his generation, it was a much larger pool of now liberated middle-class Americans, such as his Holy Cross classmates, and their children and grandchildren. Hecker knew that this required making spiritual and theological sense of America, a sense that would give meaning and direction to human work, to new opportunities for public service, and to shared responsibility for an ever more complex and interconnected common life. Catholic social thought provides rich and often untapped resources for connecting faith with shared civic and social responsibilities. But genuine love for the world has been and remains a vital and missing link. America matters, and, today, as it was for Lincoln and King and for Merton and Day, that means a love that is at best not *eros* but *agape*, love that opens hearts to everyone, for the whole human family. Today, more than ever, internationalism, love to the whole human family, is a necessary component of genuine Americanism.

I started with Thomas Merton's prayer that God be with us when we feel most lost. I close with another passage from Merton, the monk who became famous for leaving the world and its people behind and experienced years later the kind of falling in love that may be the best ground for the renewal of our lives together in

15 American priest and founder of the Paulist Fathers (1819–1888).

our common home. Whether it happens as a democratic rally for racial justice, a shared mourning for loss from a pandemic or gun violence, or at Fenway Park at another World Series, may it happen for us:

> In Louisville, at the corner of Fourth and Walnut, in the center of the shopping district, I was suddenly overwhelmed with the realization that I loved all these people, that they were mine and I theirs, that we could not be alien to one another even though we were total strangers. It was like waking from a dream of separateness, of spurious self-isolation in a special world. . . .
>
> This sense of liberation from an illusory difference was such a relief and such a joy to me that I almost laughed out loud. . . . I have the immense joy of being man, a member of a race in which God Himself became incarnate. As if the sorrows and stupidities of the human condition could overwhelm me, now that I realize what we all are. And if only everybody could realize this! But it cannot be explained. There is no way of telling people that they are all walking around shining like the sun.
>
> Then it was as if I suddenly saw the secret beauty of their hearts, the depths of their hearts where neither sin nor desire nor self-knowledge can reach, the core of their reality, the person that each one is in God's eyes. If only they could all see themselves as they really are. If only we could see each other that way all the time. There would be no more war, no more hatred, no more cruelty, no more greed. . . . But this cannot be seen, only believed and "understood" by a peculiar gift.
>
> —Thomas Merton, *Conjectures of a Guilty Bystander*

NOTES

The references to Charles Taylor come from his *The Secular Age* and from lectures available from many sources, including the Berkeley Center at Georgetown University. The Mustard Seed image, along with references to the role of doubt, the need for pastoral accompaniment, and interfaith encounter are best set forth in an informal talk delivered by Taylor in Rome and available on YouTube: https://youtu.be/152Ng0qYRIM.

The book of mine I refer to is *The Renewal of American Catholicism* (Oxford University Press, 1972). The Karl Rahner quote I find so helpful is from *The Christian Commitment* (Sheed and Ward, 1963). The Robert Bellah essay is in *Hedgehog Review,* Spring 2002.

Roots and Realities of a Priestly People

MICHAEL J. MCGRAVEY, PHD

FATHER HUGH F. Crean's approach to ministry is one marked by a collaborative spirit built on the ideas discussed at the Second Vatican Council. The Church, Crean understood, was meant to be something shared by all of the baptized, a point illuminated in *Lumen gentium,* wherein "The People of God" is expressed as all those "baptized persons who constitute the Church."[16] The Council clearly established that the Church and her hierarchy were not something that exceeded normal human life; rather, it belonged to all those baptized, reiterating a point made by Saint Augustine of Hippo (Sermon 340). Similarly, Chapter 4 of *Lumen gentium* focuses on those individuals—women and men—who have elected vocations of marriage or the single life and contribute to society and the Church in varying, collaborative ways.[17] This chapter offers a review of the historical development of the Church, focusing on the laity and their relationship to the ordained and those in positions of authority. It concludes with an examination of Vatican II and the documents that address the role of the laity in the Church before addressing Crean's emphasis on collaboration within local faith communities.

THE EARLY CHURCH: DEVELOPING A LEADERSHIP MODEL

Twelve men took up the mantle of leadership following the death of their master. These men manifested a ministry that reflects the priestly office, the prophetic office, and the kingship demonstrated in the life of Christ. Their work in this capacity included early variations of liturgical celebration, the oversight of an emerging community, and the task of developing a coherent theological

16 Richard P. McBrien, *The Church: The Evolution of Catholicism* (New York: HarperOne, 2008), 166.

17 Second Vatican Council, "Dogmatic Constitution on the Church, Lumen Gentium, 21 November, 1964," in *Vatican Council II: The Conciliar and Post Conciliar Documents (New Revised Edition),* ed. Austin Flannery (Northport, NY: Costello Publishing Company, 1996).

understanding of Christ amidst the growing counternarratives of the time.[18] Their role as Servants of Christ was not limited to their teaching and sacrificial duties but also included their responsibilities as pastors and as the ordained within the kingly office.

The Synoptics articulate a clear invitation to the Twelve, all of whom are brought into Jesus' ministry in hopes of learning more about the "divine secret, called by Mark 'the mystery of the Kingdom (4:11).'"[19] The instructions given at the end of Matthew (28:19–20) are explicit and clear: the Twelve are to minister, celebrate the Eucharist, and take on the unique role of teachers of the faith (*kerygma*).[20] Women and men in this era would work to continue a ministry they believed ordered by Christ (Mt. 28) but would soon develop a leadership model necessary for its growth and widespread geographical area. The fourth evangelist builds on the notion of the Servant of Yahweh and portrays Christ as parallel to the prophets, priests, and kings of the Hebrew Bible, notably, Jeremiah, Aaron, and Jehoiachim.[21] The Hebrew Bible model of priesthood in this case emphasizes their role as sacrificial leaders (for the Jewish Temple, sacrifices upon the altar; for the Christian community, celebrating the Eucharist at the altar). The pastoral work in John's Gospel is articulated via the Washing of the Feet (John 13:1–17) and their kingship—more appropriately, their role as shepherds—is demonstrated via Jesus' appointment as authoritative figures in the new community.[22]

---

18 Aidan Nichols, *Holy Order: Apostolic Priesthood from the New Testament to the Second Vatican Council* (Eugene, OR: Wipf & Stock, 1990), 8.

19 Ibid., 6.

20 Ibid., 7. See also, Kenan B. Osborne, *Priesthood: A History of Ordained Ministry in the Roman Catholic Church* (New York: Paulist Press, 1988), 40–41. Osborne in this case addresses the naming of "The Twelve" as well as "Apostle," both attributed to Jesus. Osborne suggests that the pastoral needs of a particular community resulted in the ministerial functions described herein.

21 Nichols, 9. Nichols continues, explaining that this Hebrew Bible connection is further elaborated on in the First Letter to Clement and the Letter to the Hebrews.

22 Nichols goes on to explain the role of the original Twelve and those added as "auxiliary apostles" or "apostolic delegates," who served the Church in a similar role; however, they were expected to maintain the tradition as Jesus' first students aged, passed, or were martyred. One such example is Timothy, appointed as a "regional vicar" for "the apostles, acting for them over areas considerably wider than a local church yet less than the Church universal . . . they had two specific tasks. . . . First, to be custodians, guardians, of the apostolic deposit . . . [and] Secondly . . . to organize the local apostolic ministry in the particular churches: that is, they were to ordain," in ibid., 16–18. Quotation, 17–18.

The priestly and kingly ministry emphasized in the ministry of Jesus found its way into the documents of Vatican II. Reflecting on the ministry of Jesus, Kenan Osborne argues that his timing was impeccable; Jesus arrived at the right time, in a situation poised for a new movement, a "charismatic movement" at a time when the population of Palestine-Israel was in need of a transformative healer and teacher.[23] Those who followed Jesus would eventually be recognized as the first bishops, with Peter as their leader.[24] These first leaders reflected the type of ministry Jesus provided: healing those most in need and preaching a similar message. Their message paralleled that of their master; it was a "message of a Jewish revival, which included a view that the end of the world would take place in the not-too-distant future."[25] Although these men and women do not fit the structure of the Church familiar to us today, those who sought renewal at Vatican II were mindful of the role ordinary people played in the life and ministry of the Church. Those who witnessed the Resurrection (1 Cor. 15) and those who were named and appointed in the Synoptic Gospels (e.g., Thomas in John 20:24) held roles important to the ministry of Jesus' group and in the community following his death. Matthias' election in Acts 1 is consistent with the leadership model chosen by Jesus: twelve men who were to work side-by-side. As the New Testament era drew to a close, this model faded, and new leaders were elected or adopted into the group. Evidence of early apostolic leadership can be seen in Paul's first letter to the Corinthians (15:3–5), in which he alludes to his time as a student (catechumen) of the faith (I Cor. 15:3–5).[26] Other leaders included those who directed the authorship of the gospels, the many women who worked tirelessly alongside Jesus, and the several named in the New Testament (e.g., Barnabas, Timothy, Philemon, Clement, Junia, and Titus).

23 Kenan B. Osborne, *Orders and Ministry: Leadership in the World Church, Theology in Global Perspective* (Maryknoll, NY: Orbis Books, 2006), 181–2.

24 Ibid., 182–3.

25 Ibid., 183.

26 Nichols, 6. The role of an apostle is further outlined in Nichols's first chapter, detailing the different scripture passages that describe their role in the Christian community. See, ibid., 12–31. In this section, Nichols delineates the role of the Twelve, ministry of the Seven, differences between local and universal leaders, apostolic auxiliaries, deacons, and more. Nichols establishes the leadership and presbyteral roles found in the early Church, relying on Luke and Acts of the Apostles along with several of the New Testament Letters.

THE POST-APOSTOLIC ERA

As the Church emerged from the apostolic era, there was a clear need to establish a leadership model that maintained an early notion of "apostolic succession." The term "apostolic succession" was aimed at combatting the Gnostics.[27] By comparison, the Christian Church established that it was universal in its teachings, no matter the locale or ethnicity it found itself within.[28] While Gnostic teachers told their audience that the orthodox teachings withheld secret teachings about Jesus, the Church countered with its presentation of "apostolic succession." Only those teachings that could be traced back to Jesus were to be accepted. "Apostolic succession does not essentially mean origin from apostles, but more importantly origin from Jesus himself."[29] More importantly, Osborne will explain, is the foundational understanding of apostolic connection, insofar as it connects the ministry of Jesus to the ministry of the Twelve and Paul to the ministry of those who took on the role of *presbyter, episkopos,* or *diakonos.* Relatedly, and on the topic of first pope, the specific role of Peter as Bishop of Rome lacks clear evidence in the New Testament and is derived from later respectable sources.[30] What is clear from the New Testament texts is that Peter was an early follower of Jesus and believed Jesus to be the Messiah but may not have fully understood the role of Christ. Moreover, the ideology of Peter according to Osborne was less conservative than that of his fellow apostle, James, but more so than that of Paul during his mission to the Gentiles.[31] The dynamic illustrated here shows the "apostolic circle," whereby

---

27 Osborne, *Priesthood: A History of Ordained Ministry in the Roman Catholic Church,* 81. Hermann Pottmeyer maintains that this remained an important aspect of the early Church; the new leadership maintained a shared heritage and line of succession to the apostles. See Hermann J. Pottmeyer, *Towards a Papacy in Communion: Perspectives from Vatican Councils I and II,* trans. Matthew J. O'Connell (New York: Crossroad Publishing Company, 1998), 24–26.

28 Bernard P. Prusak, *The Church Unfinished: Ecclesiology through the Centuries* (New York: Paulist Press, 2004), 123–4. See also Irenæus of Lyons, *Against Heresies,* ed. Alexander Roberts and James Donaldson (Jackson, MI: Ex Fontibus Company, 2017), I.X.2, 61–62.

29 Osborne, *Priesthood: A History of Ordained Ministry in the Roman Catholic Church,* 81.

30 Ibid., 82.

31 Ibid., 75.

those men tasked with the challenges of the new community traced their roots back to Jesus.[32]

As the Church grew from Emmaus and Roman Palestine, its leadership was shaped by the sharing of bread and wine between Church leaders.[33] Justin and Irenaeus of Lyons acknowledged this tradition of *koinōnia,* the sharing of Eucharist, over and against Gnosticism. Irenaeus's further contribution in this era included an emphasis on the Church's shared universal faith, reflecting the diversity in a church that would soon spread to Spain, the British Isles, Egypt, Libya, and throughout the East. Important to Irenaeus was apostolic succession insofar as this would establish a clear lineage and leadership for the young church.[34]

By its third century, the apostolic tradition was further solidified by the document *Apostolic Tradition,* commonly attributed to Hippolytus of Rome. Here, the tradition of laying on of hands is identified and recognized as ordination.

After a candidate acceptable to all had been named, the people were to assemble on a Sunday, and bishops from a neighboring church were to lay hands on him while the elders watched (*Ap. Tr.* 2). One bishop then imposed a hand and prayed that the Spirit would descend upon the new *episkopo* (*Ap. Tr.* 3).[35]

The laying on of hands and the sharing of Eucharist became fundamental to the Church's identity. By this time, the Church established a hierarchical model with a local bishop overseeing the local elders and deacons. Bishops became synonymous with the Church. During this era, the election of bishops from among the local baptized community and approved by fellow bishops was important.[36]

---

32 Pottmeyer, 26.

33 Prusak, 121. Justin Martyr's *First Apology* refers to this in light of Christian oppression and persecution.

34 For a review of Irenaeus, Clement of Rome, Hegesippus, and Tertullian, see ibid., 123–5. Tertullian's position would take on the conservative Montanist sect, which dismissed the leadership model of the Church favoring a Spirit-driven form that placed the onus on local faith communities to determine their own model; ibid., 126.

35 Ibid. Emphasis original.

36 "Cyprian and the Roman Church also agreed that members of the baptized 'faithful' were to be present and consulted at the common councils where important decisions were made (*Ep.* 17:1, 19:2, 30:5, 31:6). Their presence for the election of a new bishop was particularly crucial since they knew the life and actions of the candidates (*Ep.* 67:5). They had the power to elect worthy bishops or to refuse unworthy ones (*Ep.* 67:3)," in Prusak, 128.

Irenaeus and Tertullian understood that the bishops represented a symbol of unity while acknowledging their role as those responsible for assessing who could be included or excluded from the community. Exclusion meant that the judged was not eligible to receive the Eucharist. Those decrees and opinions would establish *orthodoxy*, or right belief, among its congregants and teachers.[37]

Rome became the center of these communal bodies by the time Augustine was elected as bishop of Hippo. Rome began to serve as the adjudicator on issues within the local churches.[38] Despite growing differences between East and West, the principle of *koinonia* remained central to the Church's growing global identity. Augustine's view of the Roman bishop was solidified in several texts (e.g., *Epistle* 43, *On Baptism* 2.1.2, *Sermon* 149.7, 295.2, and *On John* 118.4, 124.5), especially as he addressed the many controversies posed by the Donatists. The cooperation of the bishops across the growing Church was a strength in Augustine's estimation. Augustine maintained the need for him and his fellow bishops to collegially work together to address ongoing questions on the sacraments, Church teachings, and the influence of others such as Pelagius and Mani.[39] Most importantly, as bishop of Hippo, Augustine petitioned Rome on issues he felt ill-prepared to answer.[40]

Augustine and his counterparts, though helping to shape the future of Church leadership, did not neglect the role of lay women and men. The rapid expansion of these teachers of the faith provided opportunities for lay leaders such that by 500 CE, "laypeople enjoyed a variety of important roles within the church and its teaching, including leadership in liturgical and administrative structures."[41] These laymen also included a number of influential theologians

37 Ibid.

38 Ibid., 129 and 32–39.

39 Ibid., 138. Augustine relied on the analogy of husband and wife to describe the relationship between Peter and the Church. Each bishop that followed was related to and united with the bishop of Rome.

40 Ibid., 139. See, for example, Augustine, *Epistle* 209.9. Primacy continued to be the subject of future bishops and the pontiff. Prusak points to Pope Zosimus's notion that "no one could review or dispute a decision made by its bishop." Pope Boniface added his own declaration that, because the universal Church could trace its roots to Peter, it was the true Church, and because of its role as the magisterial teaching body could accept "legitimate complaints" and "its judgments could not be revised." North African bishops led by Aurelius would challenge this at Carthage, questioning how local leaders were not responsible for local issues. Popes Celestine and Sixtus III went on to maintain their ability to intervene at their leisure; ibid., 141–2.

41 Osborne, *Orders and Ministry: Leadership in the World Church*, 184.

(e.g., Tertullian, Justin, Clement of Alexandria, and Origen before his ordination in 230 CE).[42]

The legacy of the Church in an era of Roman collapse is accentuated by its survival and emergence as a community centered in the apostolic tradition, an understanding of *koinōnia,* and the celebration of the Eucharist. Augustine witnessed the looming collapse while also witnessing tremendous resiliency in the young faith he served. He was confident the Church would survive the imminent collapse of Rome because of its emphasis on unity and its propensity to love and serve.[43]

As the Church turned from Imperial Rome to a culturally and nationally divided European continent, the Church encountered new challenges. The pontiffs who rose to power were positioned in a world that demanded clarity as to their role, the role of the local bishops, and that of the ordained. As kings and princes rose to power, and the familiar refrain that their coronations were anointed by God, the princes of the Church (bishops and their subordinates) enforced their role as powerbrokers for their secular counterparts. During this time, bishops designated local parishes and assigned clergy members who were responsible for the daily practices and sacraments ("baptism, marriage, and burial . . . yearly confession and communion"[44]). As for the laity, their role became diminished and subservient to the hierarchy:

> Gradually, the role of the layperson was to follow the basic commandments of God and the Church, to confess sins and partake of the sacraments from time to time, and to receive

42 Ibid., 184–5.

43 Prusak, 175.

44 Ibid., 206. Prusak observes the emergence of parishes established out of religious communities and their monasteries who, though within the diocese of a bishop, held a great deal of autonomy; ibid., 207. As the Church entered the twelfth century, the number of priests within local parishes, those connected to parishes, and those associated with the Dominicans and Franciscans grew exponentially. The growth was positive insofar as many had access to the sacraments, and those within religious communities were especially welcomed because of their training and education. It is worth noting the mixed history those clergymen in religious orders experienced, as Prusak does. Accepted during times of crisis, these men were often the subject of papal bulls when a pontiff thought they were too autonomous or influential; ibid., 207–8.

salvation from an all-encompassing church. Accordingly, lay people were more and more excluded from leadership roles.[45]

THE MEDIEVAL CHURCH: FACING EUROPEAN CHALLENGES

The end of the thirteenth century brought about further divisions on the European continent. The administration of the Church and the governing of Europe were unified under one figure: the Pope. Archbishops and bishops administered the local communities; outside counsel made little sense for its hierarchical structure. Papal primacy and power began to take shape, presenting a case for monarchical power centralized in the papacy itself. Debates centered on papal versus national power would lead to divisions, including the Western Schism, power struggles that included several and simultaneous pontiffs who claimed their own power over believers, disputes over ecclesial property, and more.

The visible manifestation of the Church following the Reformation was the bishops and Pope, standing in contrast to the multiple emerging local leaders and pastors in the reformed traditions. The Church maintained, according to Theologian Yves Congar, the belief that the Spirit granted and approved the mode of authority.[46] This emphasis granted to the hierarchy and its authority dispensed with the ideals of the communal Church during the first few centuries, allocating the election of bishops and the priesthood from the baptized faithful to the hierarchy. "The communal idea of the church's structure was replaced by a corporative conception of it."[47]

By the time Pope Innocent III was elected pontiff, the Church had shifted in its identification of the Pope—from the "'representative of Peter' to sole 'representative of Christ'"—while also adjusting the function of the pontiff as a successor to the apostles to the "source of all power of jurisdiction."[48] The shift from representative of Peter, or vicar of Peter, was eventually adopted by Popes Innocent III and Boniface VIII. This is a clear articulation of papal supremacy over the

45 Osborne, *Orders and Ministry: Leadership in the World Church,* 187. See also Paul J. Philibert, *The Priesthood of the Faithful: Key to a Living Church* (Collegeville, MN: Liturgical Press, 2005), at 16.

46 Prusak, 248. Originally, Yves Congar, *L'église: De Saint Augustin À L'époque Moderne* (Paris: Éditions du Cerf, 1970), 381–4.

47 Pottmeyer, 29.

48 Ibid., 30.

ever-changing political landscape of the former Roman Empire.[49] Pope Innocent IV would advance the idea of "representative of Christ" by declaring that his role exceeded that of all other rulers. Innocent's declaration held that he was subject only to divine law, able to create and reject laws of the Church but not subject to the laws himself. By the end of the thirteenth century, the Church had become more monarchical than in previous centuries. The shift in the first thirteen centuries all but eliminated the connection between the laity and the ordained. The laity were removed from the operational function and theological development of the Church to the pews. The political house of cards—eventually, cardinals—took hold of a Church which aimed to serve all but benefited the rank and file.

THE NINETEENTH AND TWENTIETH CENTURIES: COUNCILS AND AUTHORITY

The Church of the nineteenth century, despite an ecclesiological shift that reemphasized Christ as prophet, king, and priest, maintained its identity as a "government" led by its Pope, bishops, and its "teaching authority, or *magisterium*."[50] What is equally concerning is the abandonment of the "'sense of the faithful,' which acknowledged the role of the entire community of believers for keeping alive the beliefs of the Church."[51] The palpable deference granted to the *magisterium* meant its foundation as a church grounded in the experiences and people of the "ordinary," including those trained as theologians, was absent from the conversation. One such critic of magisterial authority, insofar as it limited communal engagement, was John Henry Newman, particularly in his 1859 "On Consulting the Faithful in Matters of Doctrine";[52] another was Johann Adam Möhler in his *Symbolik* (1832). This stood in contrast to the ecclesial authority supported by Pope Pius IX. And despite Möhler's theological enthusiasm to return to a Church of yesteryear, Neo-Scholasticism and speculative theology took hold, delaying efforts to return to the patristics and biblical sources until the Second Vatican Council.

49 Osborne, *Orders and Ministry: Leadership in the World Church*, 186.

50 Prusak, 249–50. Emphasis original.

51 Ibid., 250.

52 Ibid. Originally, John Henry Cardinal Newman, "On Consulting the Laity," in *The Essential Newman*, ed. Vincent Ferrer Blehl (New York: Mentor-Omega Books, 1963), 274–8.

POPE JOHN XXIII AND THE SECOND VATICAN COUNCIL

John XXIII's pontificate was expected to be brief and transitional, one focused on healing "the traumas inflicted by Pius XII's long and dramatic reign."[53] John XXIII's announcement of the Second Vatican Council was shocking, to say the least. Yves Congar welcomed the Council but was adamant the Council be new and not simply a continuation of Vatican I. As a contributor, Congar focused on pastoral issues, global ethics (notably, nuclear war), Mariology, and ecumenism.[54] He also was very much concerned with the well-being of the laity and their relationship to the ordained.[55]

The newly elected pontiff faced an uphill task, the least of which involved overcoming Pius XII's curia, many of whom resisted any facets of modernism.[56] The Council would later be described by the likes of Avery Cardinal Dulles as "a center of controversy," as it attempted to address the modern world and repair perceptions of clericalism and juridicism, aiming to "rediscover" its first-century roots and heritage.

The Council sought to address the relationship between clergy and laity, to which Osborne noted the centuries of tension that existed before John XXIII's call: "Until Vatican II, the position of Church leadership was very defensive, apologetic, anti-lay, and punitive."[57] The Council's emphasis regarding the laity became a

---

53 Giuseppe Alberigo, "The Announcement of the Council: From the Security of the Fortress to the Lure of the Quest," in *The History of Vatican II,* ed. Giuseppe Alberigo and Joseph A. Komonchak (Maryknoll, NY: Orbis Books, 1995), 2.

54 Ibid., 35. Pius XII's *Humani Generis* (1950) demonstrated the *Magisterium*'s position regarding their theological initiatives, asserting the role of the Church as the definitive teaching authority. Congar and other *la nouvelle théologie* scholars were rejected under the previous pontiff. Congar, Henri de Lubac, Louis Bouyer, and Mannes D. Koster were limited in their role as theologians by Pius XII. Their work and ideas would be influential in many of the outcomes of the Second Vatican Council. See, for example, Gabriel Daly, "Catholicism and Modernity," *Journal of the American Academy of Religion* 53, no. 4 (1985): at 774; and Paul Lakeland, "*Lumen gentium:* The Unfinished Business," *New Blackfriars* 1026, no. 90 (2008): 146–7; and Philibert, 56. Chapter 4 of Philibert's *The Priesthood of the Faithful* outlines in detail Congar's involvement and contributions at the Second Vatican Council, following decades of humiliation by Pius XII and his counterparts in Rome.

55 For example, in Philibert, 19.

56 Alberigo, in *The History of Vatican II,* 5.

57 Kenan Osborne, "Who Did What in the Church in the Second Millennium?" in *Lay Ministry in the Catholic Church: Visioning Church Ministry through the Wisdom of the Past,* ed. Richard W. Miller II (Ligouri, MO: Liguori, 2005), 47.

focus for the Council. One of the seminal documents, *Lumen gentium* (*Dogmatic Constitution on the Church,* 1964), sought to address the Church in contemporary society. Pottmeyer adds, "it takes an important step forward, for it reflects upon the original theology and order of the church in the first millennium."[58]

Chapter 2 of the document presents all women and men as beneficiaries of creation, transcending "all times and all racial boundaries."[59] Those who have been baptized and those who have been ordained are subsequently referred to as a priestly people, wherein they share in the priesthood of Christ (a major theme of the Council).[60] A shared responsibility to care for one another and the Church is derived from this section:

> All the disciples of Christ, persevering in prayer and praising God (cf. Acts 2:42-47), should present themselves as a sacrifice, living, holy and pleasing to God (cf. Rom. 12:1). They should everywhere on earth bear witness to Christ and give an answer to everyone who asks a reason for the hope of an eternal life which is theirs (cf. 1 Pet. 3:15). Though they differ essentially and not only in degree, the common priesthood of the faithful and the ministerial or hierarchical are none the less ordered one to another; each in its own proper way shares in the one priesthood of Christ. The ministerial priest, by the sacred power that he has, forms, and rules the priestly people; in the person of Christ, he effects the

58 Pottmeyer, 111. Pottmeyer addresses both the strengths of the document (it addresses the clerical and judicial tendencies of the Church) as well as its weakness (it does little to address the modern world). For a brief presentation on the drafting of *Lumen gentium,* see Richard R. Gaillardetz, *The Church in the Making: Lumen gentium, Christus Dominus, Orientalium ecclesiarum* (New York: Paulist Press, 2006), 8–27.

59 "Dogmatic Constitution on the Church, *Lumen gentium,* 21 November, 1964," *Vatican Council II: The Conciliar and Post Conciliar Documents (New Revised Edition),* §9.

60 Ibid., §10. Relatedly, Crean stated the following: "Since Vatican II a new focus on ministry has emerged in theological reflection and pastoral practice. This has contributed to a historical recovery of our church roots and a shift in theological perspective. It is the result of many new or rediscovered insights that the council brought to light. Vatican II represented a culmination of biblical, theological, and liturgical research that had been going on for decades. . . . It crystallized more than eighty years of papal pronouncements on social justice. . . . If Vatican I (1869–1870) was the council of the papacy, Vatican II was the council of the laity," in Crean, 6.

> eucharistic sacrifice and offers it to God in the name of all the people. The faithful indeed, by virtue of their royal priesthood, participate in the offering of the Eucharist. They exercise that priesthood, too, by the reception of the sacraments, prayer and thanksgiving, the witness of a holy life, abnegation and active charity.[61]

The bishops were clear: the Church was intended to be available and accessible to all people.[62] The responsibility to care for the Church and one another is one that falls on the shoulders of all, the laity and ordained.[63]

There is a clear shift in the language of the Council versus the preceding era in the Church, which emphasized the place and tasks of the ordained. For all of those baptized within the Church, *Lumen gentium* emphasizes the place of the Eucharist and its accessibility to all those eligible to receive it. It maintains the role of the ordained insofar as they oversee the celebration of the Eucharist, but it is the whole community who gathers to celebrate and partake. *Lumen gentium* encourages the growth of and expression of the "domestic Church," wherein parents share their faith with their children who are too young for the sacraments.[64] Thus, *Lumen gentium* outlines the place of all women and men within the Church in a shared, common priesthood, acknowledging the diversity and gifts among the faithful. "In virtue of this catholicity each part contributes its own gifts to other parts and to the whole Church, so that the whole and each of the parts are strengthened by the common effort to attain to fullness in unity. Hence it is that the People of God is not only an assembly of various peoples, but is made up of different ranks."[65]

Additionally, *Lumen gentium* observes the value of urban and suburban parishes, whether urban or suburban, no matter the ethnicity. Section 13

---

61 "Dogmatic Constitution on the Church, *Lumen gentium*, 21 November, 1964," *Vatican Council II: The Conciliar and Post Conciliar Documents (New Revised Edition)*, §10.

62 Osborne, *Orders and Ministry: Leadership in the World Church*, 173.

63 Ibid. Emphasis original.

64 "Dogmatic Constitution on the Church, *Lumen gentium*, 21 November, 1964," *Vatican Council II: The Conciliar and Post Conciliar Documents (New Revised Edition)*, §11.

65 Ibid., §13.

addresses the diversity of the local and universal Church, observing the commonality women and men share despite cultural, linguistic, or national differences; each contributes in her or his own way. Thus, "All [women and] men are called to this catholic unity which prefigures and promotes universal peace."[66]

Chapter 2 concludes with observations of those who are baptized; those who have access to the Gospels yet refrain from embracing the tradition; and those who are Jewish, Muslim, and otherwise. Humanity's shared existence and God's willing embodiment is identified within *Lumen gentium* as the shared heritage between the women and men as participants in creation. For those who are Jewish, the Church acknowledges the long-standing covenant. For those who are Muslim, the Church respects the faith as an Abrahamic tradition born in the Arabian Peninsula with knowledge of and respect for Judaism and Christianity.[67]

Chapter 3 reinforces collegiality within the bishops, alluding to a reaffirmation of the ancient Church's model of a hierarchy that sought to solve issues of the faith, albeit with limitations for the laity. *Lumen gentium*'s sections 19 and 23 specifically address collegiality, primacy, apostolic succession, and the teaching authority of the Roman Pontiff, who works collaboratively with those appointed bishops (successors of the apostles).[68] By addressing these topics, the document established a hierarchical model for itself and the baptized within the faith, while also addressing those who questioned the often ridiculed and misunderstood teachings on infallibility and collegiality among the bishops. Together, the College of Bishops and the Pope serve the Church when addressing issues of the faith; neither can serve

66 Ibid., §13.

67 Ibid., §§15–16.

68 Ibid., §18. Prusak addresses the collegiality called for in *Lumen gentium,* writing in part, "Contemporary scholarship recognizes that there was a development in leadership structures—moving from the Twelve and the disciples called by Jesus, to a 'pluriformity' of diverse types of leadership in the earliest postresurrection communities, to the eighties' universalizing of a collegial leadership pattern interchangeably called overseers/elders (*episkopoi/presbyteroi*) working with the group known as deacons, and finally, at the beginning of the second century, to the emergence of the *mono-episkopos* (or bishop) presiding over the elders and deacons. . . . In discussing the role of bishops within the Church, Chapter 3 [of *LUMEN GENTIUM*] reflects an intense concern for specifying their relationship to the Pope." The clarification here, Prusak continues, is intended to defend the role of the Pope and his primacy, while also addressing the collegiality apparent throughout the history of the Church; in, Prusak, 284–5. Also, Pottmeyer, 113–5.

without the other.[69] Likewise, as the document goes on to address, those serving local dioceses as priests and deacons are recognized because of their collaborative roles: serving those in need, administering applicable sacraments, and bringing their gifts to parishes and dioceses.[70]

The fourth chapter of *Lumen gentium* examines the laity in relationship to those tasked with the administration of the Church and her sacraments:

> The term "laity" is here understood to mean all the faithful except those in Holy Orders and those who belong to a religious state approved by the Church. That is, the faithful who by Baptism are incorporated into Christ, are placed in the people of God, and in their own way share the priestly, prophetic and kingly functions of Christ, and to the best of their ability carry on the mission of the whole Christian people in the Church and in the world.[71]

Shaped by the Catholic Action movement in Western Europe and the United States (1930s–1950s), the Church sought to better involve all people, notably its laity. Several theologians, including Congar, Karl Rahner, Marie-Dominique Chenu, and Jean Daniélou, explored what this relationship should look like, encouraging a much more positive engagement between laity and Church leaders.[72]

Referring to their unique place within the Church, existing solely in the secular world, the laity are encouraged to bring their gifts to the life of the faith community while also sharing their faith with those outside their parish and faith life. All baptized are called to work together, equally and with the same

---

69 "Dogmatic Constitution on the Church, *Lumen Gentium,* 21 November, 1964," *Vatican Council II: The Conciliar and Post Conciliar Documents (New Revised Edition),* §22.

70 See ibid., §§28–29. Additionally, Hans Urs von Balthasar, *The Office of Peter and the Structure of the Church* (San Francisco: Ignatius Press, 1986), 220ff.

71 "Dogmatic Constitution on the Church, *Lumen Gentium,* 21 November, 1964," *Vatican Council II: The Conciliar and Post Conciliar Documents (New Revised Edition),* §31. Clear in this section is the Church's insistence that clergy also work and exist within the secular world; they are not removed from or immune to the realities of secular influence. This is further reiterated in Second Vatican Council, "Gaudium et spes (Pastoral Constitution on the Church in the Modern World)," in *Vatican Council II: The Conciliar and Post Conciliar Documents (New Revised Edition),* ed. Austin Flannery (Northport, NY: Costello Publishing Company, 1965), §43. For more on baptism and the laity, see Philibert, 22–38.

72 Gaillardetz, 52–53.

purpose, seeking to create a world that mimics the Kingdom of God.[73] This is not a task that is granted haphazardly or via the hierarchy; rather, this is designated to an individual due to her or his baptism. The challenge, as Prusak alludes, is the connection between the "lay apostolate" and the "apostolate of the hierarchy," specifically, how the two are asked to work together.[74] Moreover, Chapter 4 insists the laity

> recognize their inner nature, the value and the ordering of the whole of creation. . . . By their secular activity they help one another achieve greater holiness of life, so that the world may be filled with the spirit of Christ and may the more effectively attain its destiny in justice, in love and in peace. The laity enjoy a principal role in the universal fulfillment of this task.[75]

This is not a definition of the laity—something the Council intentionally avoided, hoping to avoid a typology that might have occurred with a set description.[76] The "principle role" here is to bring the life of the faith into the secular, addressing "the institutions and conditions of the world when the latter are an inducement to sin," seeking remedies where and when possible.[77] At the conclusion of Chapter 4, *Lumen gentium* articulates the need for lay women and men to work for the benefit of society and the Church by working with pastors on various issues, alluding to the principle of subsidiarity. "The pastors, indeed, should recognize and promote the dignity and responsibility of the laity in the Church. . . . Indeed, they [pastors] should give them [the laity] the courage to

73 "Dogmatic Constitution on the Church, *Lumen gentium*, 21 November, 1964," in *Vatican Council II: The Conciliar and Post Conciliar Documents (New Revised Edition)*, §§32–33.

74 Prusak, 293.

75 "Dogmatic Constitution on the Church, *Lumen gentium*, 21 November, 1964," in *Vatican Council II: The Conciliar and Post Conciliar Documents (New Revised Edition)*, §36. Gaillardetz points to the work of Giovanni Magnani and his assertion that the Council's documents intended to (1) contrast the laity to that of clergy (*Lumen gentium* §31) and (2) reiterate the role of the laity in the Church and secular world. See Gaillardetz, 53–54.

76 Gaillardetz, 54.

77 "Dogmatic Constitution on the Church, *Lumen gentium*, 21 November, 1964," in *Vatican Council II: The Conciliar and Post Conciliar Documents (New Revised Edition)*, §36.

undertake works in their own initiative."[78] This relationship between pastors and congregants seeks to fulfill the mission of the Church, creating a better society centered on the Kingdom of God.

The goals and ideals of Vatican II and, specifically, *Lumen gentium* remain elusive with respect to documents and the system of governance the Church has maintained. Dulles notes the shift in lay ministries since the Council's close and its principles' adoption:

> Since the council we have seen in the church a great increase in lay ministries, not only the canonically erected ministries of reader and acolyte, but also ministries of teaching, music, social action, counseling, and even the distribution of Holy Communion. There has been a great and welcome influx of laymen and laywomen into theology. . . . In a period of diminishing vocations to the clerical and religious life it is urgent that lay persons assume greater responsibility than ever for the faith and life of the church.[79]

These new ministries have raised several questions pertaining to the authority of the laity in connection to the clergy of their local parish and diocese. The Church has had a difficult time adjusting to the post-conciliar shifts and the inclusion of women and men who are not ordained.[80] Nevertheless, lingering clericalism, despite recent dark chapters in the Church here and abroad, remains the "dominant, operative theology," according to Osborne.[81]

Other documents that grant attention to the laity include the Council's *Constitution on the Sacred Liturgy* (*Sacrosanctum concilium*, 1963), the *Decree on the Laity* (*Apostolicam actuositatem*, 1965), the *Decree on the Pastoral Office*

---

78 Ibid., §37.

79 Dulles, 28.

80 Gerard Mannion addresses this top-down hierarchical authority found in the Church wherein he offers several examples of this tension in his 2002 essay, "What Do We Mean by 'Authority'?" See Gerard Mannion, "What Do We Mean by 'Authority'?" in *Authority in the Roman Catholic Church: Theory and Practice*, ed. Bernard Hoose (Burlington, VT: Ashgate Publishing, 2002), 19–36 at 22.

81 Osborne, in *Lay Ministry in the Catholic Church: Visioning Church Ministry through the Wisdom of the Past*, 48.

of Bishops in the Church (*Christus Dominus*, 1965), and the *Decree on the Church's Missionary Activity* (*Ad gentes*, 1965). *Sacrosanctum concilium* (*SC*), for example, emphasized the connection between the ordained and laity, stating clearly that the celebration of the liturgy is for all (not exclusive to the clergy). The Council's Decree on the Apostolate of the Laity (*Apostolicam actuositatem*) does reaffirm *Lumen gentium*, insofar as observing the important role the laity has in the secular world. In this arena, the laity are encouraged to speak freely (and, in turn, share their faith). All of the baptized are asked to be "active participants in the worship, the mission, [and] the entire life of the Church."[82] *SC* expanded opportunities for the laity to serve the Church and the liturgy, offering opportunities for men and women the roles of catechists, liturgical and eucharistic ministers, and more.[83] This was a drastic shift from the 1917 Code of Canon Law, which limited these roles to the clergy (though dioceses outside the United States have installed many women and men in these roles as "official ministers" within their parish).[84] These responsibilities were echoed in *Apostolicam actuositatem*, where the laity are reminded of their place in the secular world, where they are asked to spread the virtues of the faith in places common to them (work, schools, and social environments). Catholic Charities, the Knights of Peter Claver, etc., are all examples where the laity are encouraged to and will find opportunities to serve the local Church in organizations that encourage lay participation.

Finally, the *Pastoral Constitution on the Church in the Modern World* (*Gaudium et spes*, 1965) focused on the role of the laity *with* the clergy working together to promote and encourage the growth of the Church. Yet, as Fox writes, "When the dominant image was the Church as institution and hierarchy," as was the case outlined earlier, "the Church was seen as something other than the world, confronting it, over it. But as People of God, the Church is in the world and participates in its movement. '[The] faithful are not so much sent to it as find

---

82 Zeni Fox, *New Ecclesial Ministry: Lay Professionals Serving the Church* (Kansas City, MO: Sheed & Ward, 1997), 178. See also, Éamonn Fitzgibbon, "Clericalization of the Laity: A Prescient Warning of Pope Francis for the Catholic Church in Ireland," *Irish Theological Quarterly* 85, no. 1 (2020). Crean lists several of these changes and ministries since the close of the Council; see Crean, 12.

83 Philibert, 17.

84 Fox, 179.

themselves in it and from part of it. They are simply asked to be Christians in all that they are.'"[85]

The changes pronounced at the Council—including the liturgical changes, specifically those relating to the ministries of the Church—meant Paul VI and the College of Bishops were tasked with changing existing documents, structures, and policies. Notably, the liturgical texts were ordered to be revised as quickly as possible. The Church also faced the new leadership and ministerial responsibilities of the laity, primarily men, who were invited to serve the Church in new ways, as lectors, acolytes, and more. Paul VI's view on Church ministry and evangelization continued in his 1975 *Evangelii nuntiandi,* where he observes the role of the laity in the "temporal world." And though the temporal, secular world encourages new (social) communities—including in the online era—Paul VI discourages the creation of new ecclesial communities and the building up of existing ones; this remains the task of the pastors.[86]

Fox also explores the importance of the Revised Code of Canon Law, which aims to further implement the ideas of Vatican II. Canons 517, 228, and 230-1 are referenced as ones that address qualified laypersons in various roles within the Church. The Code of Canon Law provides guidance for those ministries and roles within the Church that had not been envisioned at the Council and in the 1960s. As we continue deep into the information age and social media, one can conceive of even more ministries evolving to help serve the Church, especially as it continues to shrink in many Western communities and in many facets of its existence (from the ordained to the regular attendees).

In 1987, the Catholic bishops in the United States engaged in conversations with over two hundred thousand laypersons, who in turn would represent the concerns of the Church before the synod gathering in Rome. The goal was to address the changes in lay ministry and diocesan engagement in the twenty years following the close of the Council.[87] At the synod gathering,

85 Fox, 190–91. Original quote in "Session Vi: The Laity," in *Vatican II: An Interfaith Appraisal,* ed. John H. Miller (Notre Dame: University of Notre Dame Press, 1966), 246.

86 Fox, 194–5.

87 Fox, 198. Though Fox's text is focused on ministry in the United States, he observes that similar themes and concerns were addressed in other lay/bishop conversations around the globe.

bishops discussed the growing ministries among laypersons, granting special attention to "the charisms and services proper to women." The multicultural synod also illustrated the diverse ministries offered by women and men around the world (e.g., Zaire's "mokambi, laymen responsible for a parish").[88] Similar efforts have taken place by way of synods during the pontificate of Francis. New ecclesial movements that have emphasized the laity's involvement in the modern Church have been explored by theologians such as Massimo Faggioli.[89]

COLLABORATIVE MINISTRY IN TODAY'S CHURCH

This overview of the tense history between the Church's hierarchy and laypersons points to the many opportunities that exist for the Church in the twenty-first century. Many women and men have undertaken ministerial and administrative roles, despite the shrinking reality of our parish communities. Organizations such as Georgetown University's Center for Applied Research in the Apostolate and separately the Pew Forum have tracked data which reflects changes in the Church since the Second Vatican Council. Most of us are familiar with these trends—the declines in attendance, religious identity, charitable contributions, and clergy. The latter trend has necessitated the participation of lay ministers in the daily operations of the parishes and dioceses. Tasks which had been previously delegated to clergy and women religious have now been filled by lay women and men; directors of faith formation or religious education, administrators of parochial schools, and presidents of colleges and high schools have largely transitioned to lay leaders. The recognition of these faithful women and men as leaders within the Church and her institutions fulfills many of the goals and objectives found in *Lumen gentium* and elsewhere. This secular training has in fact helped the Church as it wrestles with the realities of the twenty-first century.

---

88 Ibid., 201. Fox also observes the question as to whether women could serve as deacons and non-ordained ministries, ibid., 202.

89 See, for example, Massimo Faggioli, *Sorting out Catholicism: A Brief History of the New Ecclesial Movements* (Collegeville, MN: Liturgical Press, 2014).

REFLECTIONS ON CREAN'S SEMINAL INSIGHTS FORTY YEARS LATER

Father Hugh Crean's participation in the 1984 Future of Ministry in the Church of New England Symposium led to the participation of his presented paper, "Roots and Realities of a Priestly People."[90] Crean's essay reflects much of what has been presented in this chapter: the Church's struggles as it faced early internal and external opposition, the need to develop leaders to carry on the apostolic tradition, the development of a hierarchy that limited the engagement of lay women and men, and the eventual call for the Second Vatican Council to address the needs of the Church in the modern world. To this last point, echoing the strides of the Council addressed herein, Crean wrote, "For the past twenty years, an exciting and challenging era of Church history has unfolded with the publication of the documents of Vatican II and reflection on them."[91] The focus of his essay was threefold: on the priesthood, on baptism, and on ecclesiology.

Addressing the priesthood of all believers was at the core of the Second Vatican Council, but, as Crean observes, "the full implications for the life and ministry of all believers who share this priesthood are yet to be made clear—a challenge to the Church of our time."[92] The ordained are charged by Crean to assist in "facilitating" opportunities for lay women and men to serve in these roles. The ordained, asked to "listen and share" with the laity, are likewise reminded of their duty to upload the priestly, cultic tradition of the Hebrew Bible. While Crean observes the biblical roots' ancient priesthood and the priesthood of Christ, the observations made through Vatican II about the priesthood of all believers are especially important:

> The reaffirmation of the unique priesthood of Jesus Christ and the new probing concerning the specificity of the ordained priesthood are important outgrowths of Vatican II. However, the renewed

---

90 Hugh F. Crean, "Roots and Realities of a Priestly People," in *The Future of Ministry: The New England Symposium Papers*, ed. Joseph P. Sinwell and Billie Poon (New York: William H. Sadlier, Inc., 1985), 13–31.

91 Ibid., 16.

92 Ibid.

> emphasis on the priesthood of all believers is especially significant for our investigation of the subject of ministry in the Church. Through baptism, members of the believing community are empowered to minister to God's people.[93]

The Council's "new emphasis on baptism" goes beyond the understanding of the sacrament as that which removes sin and welcomes an individual into the life of the Church. Though often administered by an ordained member of the Church, the sacrament itself is "rooted in Christ," and shared among all believers.[94] The USCCB (U.S. Conference of Catholic Bishops) 1980 reflection, "The Laity: Called and Gifted," further promoted the sacrament of baptism (and confirmation), celebrating the Council's renewed emphasis, while acknowledging the sacrament as an important initiation into the life and ministry of the Church.[95]

Lumen gentium and other documents from the Council have emerged, providing opportunities for the laity and ordained to work collaboratively on shared projects.[96] The work is multifaceted: "parish councils, administrative and educational boards, evangelization committees, social action groups, sacramental preparation efforts . . . catechetical programs," and more.[97] Tasks previously reserved for the ordained were opened and encouraged in the Council's documents (e.g., eucharistic ministers, lectors, music ministers, prayer and scripture group leaders, etc.),[98] recalling many of the leadership roles listed earlier in this chapter, building on the many gifts the laity may offer. The opportunities to serve the Church are many and focus on both the liturgical life and the social outreach programs of the local parishes and dioceses: "[The laity celebrate] the presence of God, create community, serve the suffering world, and proclaim

---

93 Ibid., 17.

94 Ibid.

95 Ibid., 17–18.

96 Crean refers to Avery Cardinal Dulles's *Models of the Church* (1974) and Bernard Cooke's *Ministry to Word and Sacrament* (1975) as examples of ecclesiological works.

97 Crean, "Roots and Realities of a Priestly People," in *The Future of Ministry: The New England Symposium Papers*, 19.

98 Ibid.

the Good News in countless ordinary actions of living, and in these actions they contribute to the ministry of the Church."[99]

Crean maintains three traits which he observes are "indispensable" for collaborative work between the ordained and laity. First is "Faith in God and in others," which centers the work of both aspects of this partnership. Second is "Love of the Church." Despite the challenges and dark episodes, there is a common and shared admiration of the Church that emerged in the decades after the Council. And third is the need to be aware of how language impacts relationships; language of support is much more beneficial than divisive language. These lay women and men are not ordained, nor professionals hired to direct religious education programs, after-school programs, faith formation classes, etc.; rather, they are often volunteers, willing to add to their already busy lives by serving as lectors, teachers, summer camp leaders, sponsors for Rite of Christian Initiation of Adults (RICA) candidates, and more.[100]

Crean grants special attention, rightly so, to the role of women within the Church, observing the shift in the 1980s of women in the workplace. In short, women began to take on new roles "in business, government, and industry," and have continued to do so.[101] And we might add that women have taken on leadership roles in health care, higher education, government, and in the military. Many of these women have continued to be active members within their local parishes, serving as volunteers and extraordinary ministers. Though commissions have been organized to address women's ordination (as deacons and priests), the clergy remains all male, but this should not discourage laywomen from participating in various aspects of the Church. "The Church needs to develop an increased sensitivity to the role of women, because the Church benefits so greatly from their ministry."[102] Post-Vatican II theological programs have encouraged the work of feminist theologians such as Elizabeth Johnson, Elisabeth Schüssler Fiorenza, M. Shawn Copeland, Lisa Sowle Cahill, and more.

---

99 Ibid., 21.

100 Especially, Crean, "Elms College - February 25, 1991."

101 Crean, "Roots and Realities of a Priestly People," in *The Future of Ministry: The New England Symposium Papers*, 22.

102 Ibid. Several of these ministries are listed in Crean, "Elms College - February 25, 1991," 2.

Although Crean wrote this essay in the mid-1980s, he made it very clear that the nonordained and ordained must work together. The decades that have followed the pontificate of John Paul II, however, were far from glamorous. Scandal and cover-ups dominated the headlines in the waning days of his papacy and would be mirrored by headlines in the era of his successors, Benedict XVI and Francis. Despite scandal, challenges, closings and mergers, financial troubles, and more, the nonordained ministries within the Church are nevertheless called to respond to the needs of the times.[103] Though the Council opened avenues for lay ministers in the liturgy and parish, it could not anticipate the advances of technology, its prevalence in our lives, and the portability of information in our pockets. Today, the ordained and nonordained face increasingly and rapidly developing technologies that demand a rethinking of ministry to those whose communication format relies heavily on those portable devices.[104]

This requires, as Crean observed in 1985, collaboration between invested partners (ordained and nonordained). As the laity continues to face the challenges posed to the Church in the beginning of this century, the relationship with the laity is even more important. Initiatives such as Safe Environment and Virtus programs aim to protect young children from situations of vulnerability. The Church continues to explore programs and hold conversations with parents and children on issues of safety. Likewise, Catholic school faculty, staff, and administrators are required to participate in safe-training sessions, while some have called for seminary education to include similar education for those men on the path to ordination.[105]

Dark episodes in the life of the Church are met with those willing to work to rebuild the faith—and not just those in an administrative or ordained roles; this task also falls on the shoulders of lay women and men who are recognized for their paid and unpaid tasks within the Church. "Renewal," writes Crean, "is a slow

103 Hugh Crean observes the selfishness of some who are more inclined to enjoy the suffering of others versus the collaboration he cherished in his own work and in the spirit of *Lumen gentium* and the Council (in Hugh F. Crean, *Reflection on Corpus Christi* [Diocese of Springfield, Massachusetts: 1996]).

104 See, for example, Heidi A. Campbell, "Introduction: Studying Digital Ecclesiology: How Churches Are Being Informed by Digital Media and Cultures," *Ecclesial Practices* 7 (2020). In his 1991 public lecture at Elms College, Crean dared to imagine where the Church would be in the year 2000, though he leaves the speculative advancements of technology; in Crean, "Elms College - February 25, 1991," 3.

105 For example, Norbert Ebisike, "Clergy Abuse: What Is to Be Done?" *Society* 57 (2020): 6–7.

process," and though he was addressing the tensions that existed in the 1980s, the sentiment rings true today.[106] Crean calls on the institutional Church to recognize the values and virtues of the laity, as intended in *Lumen gentium* and elsewhere. Mindful of the gifts of the laity and the pastoral responsibility of the Church as a whole, Crean reminds the reader that each participant is asked to share her or his gifts to share the Gospel with friends and family in day-to-day life.

REFERENCES

Alberigo, Giuseppe. "The Announcement of the Council: From the Security of the Fortress to the Lure of the Quest." In *The History of Vatican II*, edited by Giuseppe Alberigo and Joseph A. Komonchak, vol 1. Maryknoll, NY: Orbis Books, 1995.

Balthasar, Hans Urs von. *The Office of Peter and the Structure of the Church.* San Francisco: Ignatius Press, 1986.

Campbell, Heidi A. "Introduction: Studying Digital Ecclesiology: How Churches Are Being Informed by Digital Media and Cultures." *Ecclesial Practices* 7 (2020): 1–10.

Congar, Yves. *L'église: De Saint Augustin À L'époque Moderne.* Paris: Éditions du Cerf, 1970.

Council, Second Vatican. "Dogmatic Constitution on the Church, *Lumen gentium*, 21 November, 1964." In *Vatican Council II: The Conciliar and Post Conciliar Documents (New Revised Edition)*, edited by Austin Flannery, vol I. Northport, NY: Costello Publishing Company, 1996.

Council, Second Vatican. "Gaudium et spes (Pastoral Constitution on the Church in the Modern World)." In *Vatican Council II: The Conciliar and Post Conciliar Documents (New Revised Edition)*, edited by Austin Flannery, vol 1, 903–1001. Northport, NY: Costello Publishing Company, 1965.

106 Crean, "Roots and Realities of a Priestly People," in *The Future of Ministry: The New England Symposium Papers*, 25.

Crean, Hugh F. *Elms College—February 25, 1991.* Diocese of Springfield, MA, 1991.

Crean, Hugh F. *Reflection on Corpus Christi.* Diocese of Springfield, MA, 1996.

Crean, Hugh F. "Roots and Realities of a Priestly People." In *The Future of Ministry: The New England Symposium Papers,* edited by Joseph P. Sinwell and Billie Poon. New York: William H. Sadlier, Inc., 1985.

Daly, Gabriel. "Catholicism and Modernity." *Journal of the American Academy of Religion* 53, no. 4 (1985): 773–96.

Dulles, Avery. *The Reshaping of Catholicism: Current Challenges in the Theology of Church.* New York: Harper & Row, 1988.

Ebisike, Norbert. "Clergy Abuse: What Is to Be Done?" *Society* 57 (2020): 3–8.

Faggioli, Massimo. *Sorting out Catholicism: A Brief History of the New Ecclesial Movements.* Collegeville, MN: Liturgical Press, 2014.

Fitzgibbon, Éamonn. "Clericalization of the Laity: A Prescient Warning of Pope Francis for the Catholic Church in Ireland." *Irish Theological Quarterly* 85, no. 1 (2020): 16–34.

Fox, Zeni. *New Ecclesial Ministry: Lay Professionals Serving the Church.* Kansas City, MO: Sheed & Ward, 1997.

Gaillardetz, Richard R. *The Church in the Making: Lumen gentium, Christus Dominus, Orientalium ecclesiarum.* New York: Paulist Press, 2006.

Lakeland, Paul. "*Lumen gentium:* The Unfinished Business." *New Blackfriars* 1026, no. 90 (2008): 146–62.

Lyons, Irenæus of. *Against Heresies,* edited by Alexander Roberts and James Donaldson. Jackson, MI: Ex Fontibus Company, 2017.

Mannion, Gerard. "What Do We Mean by 'Authority'?" In *Authority in the Roman Catholic Church: Theory and Practice,* edited by Bernard Hoose. Burlington, VT: Ashgate Publishing, 2002.

McBrien, Richard P. *The Church: The Evolution of Catholicism.* New York: HarperOne, 2008.

Newman, John Henry Cardinal. "On Consulting the Laity." In *The Essential Newman,* edited by Vincent Ferrer Blehl, 274–8. New York: Mentor-Omega Books, 1963.

Nichols, Aidan. *Holy Order: Apostolic Priesthood from the New Testament to the Second Vatican Council.* Eugene, OR: Wipf & Stock, 1990.

Osborne, Kenan. "Who Did What in the Church in the Second Millennium?" In *Lay Ministry in the Catholic Church: Visioning Church Ministry through the Wisdom of the Past,* edited by Richard W. Miller II. Ligouri, MO: Liguori, 2005.

Osborne, Kenan B. *Orders and Ministry: Leadership in the World Church.* Theology in Global Perspective, edited by Peter C. Phan. Maryknoll, NY: Orbis Books, 2006.

Osborne, Kenan B. *Priesthood: A History of Ordained Ministry in the Roman Catholic Church.* New York: Paulist Press, 1988.

Philibert, Paul J. *The Priesthood of the Faithful: Key to a Living Church.* Collegeville, MN: Liturgical Press, 2005.

Pius XI. "Quadragesimo anno," 1931. Accessed September 7, 2021. https://www.vatican.va/content/pius-xi/en/encyclicals/documents/hf_p-xi_enc_19310515_quadragesimo-anno.html

Pottmeyer, Hermann J. *Towards a Papacy in Communion: Perspectives from Vatican Councils I and II,* translated by Matthew J. O'Connell. New York: Crossroad Publishing Company, 1998.

Prusak, Bernard P. *The Church Unfinished: Ecclesiology through the Centuries.* New York: Paulist Press, 2004.

"Session VI: The Laity." In *Vatican II: An Interfaith Appraisal,* edited by John H. Miller. Notre Dame: University of Notre Dame Press, 1966.

Father Hugh Crean: Master Builder of Bridges

MARY B. JOHNSON, SNDdeN, PhD

THE PUBLICATION DATE of this book is 2022, the sixtieth anniversary of the beginning of the Second Vatican Council (1962–1965) and the sixtieth anniversary of the ordination to the priesthood of Father Hugh Crean. These historic milestones frame the challenge of today as Pope Francis works to refocus the Church on the theological and pastoral vision of that authoritative Council. At this time, in particular, it is important to recall and learn from women and men who were shaped by the Council's vision and who grew to embody its spirit. Father Hugh is a wonderful example of a person who lived, preached, and taught the letter and spirit of the Council.

A talk given by Father Hugh in the 1980s illustrates this:

> On December 8, 1965, Vatican II had ended, but it was just beginning. The Spirit of God whispered deeply into the being and consciousness of the Church. The invitation to renewal, to more complete involvement of all the members of the Church, had been uttered, and like Abraham we go—alive and young and fresh to a place the Spirit will show us. We are a proud and privileged people; we love our Church and what it calls us to become as we move to the year 2000. As we contemplate the wonder and challenge of our involved ministering Catholic life, we may ask:
>
> If not this . . . what?
> If not now . . . when?
> If not us . . . whom?

The citation above includes the themes of Father Hugh's priesthood that continue to inspire us: his exquisite attentiveness to and trust in the Spirit of God, his love for the Church, his fidelity to the invitation of Vatican II for the renewal of the Church and "the complete involvement of all the members of the Church," his vision of "our involved ministering Catholic life," and his call to action to each one of us to go as a Church to a "place the Spirit will show us."

The Council took place at the beginning of Father Hugh's first assignment after ordination. From 1962 to 1969, he served as associate pastor of Saint Michael's parish in East Longmeadow, Massachusetts. That assignment spanned the Council and the first four post-Conciliar years. Thus, the Second Vatican Council was the bedrock of Father Hugh's priesthood.

After the completion of his first assignment, Father Hugh was sent to the University of Louvain in Belgium for graduate studies for a period of four years. His educational background and success could have easily placed him in an academic role throughout his priesthood, where his gifts of scholarship and teaching would be focused in a college classroom and his pastoral gifts dedicated to those members of the campus community. Indeed, after completing his doctoral degree, Father Hugh taught theology for six years, from 1973 to 1979, at the College of Our Lady of the Elms in Chicopee, Massachusetts. Students of his still recall his wonderful lectures and his graceful presence on the campus.

Father Hugh's calling, however, as a diocesan priest rather than a member of a religious order, allowed him to make parish life a significant focus of his concern and source of meaning for him. When Father Hugh was asked why he had chosen to be a diocesan priest, he said, "I wanted to keep my feet firmly planted among the people."

It was that calling that moved him to engage with the joys and sorrows of all the people of a parish and to teach beyond the walls of a classroom. These moves allowed him to share the letter and spirit of the Council more broadly. His personal charism allowed him to relate to people across all the lines that often divide people from one another. He was cosmopolitan, not parochial, in his outlook and his interactions. His attitudes and behavior gave witness to his belief that the world was not to be feared but to be embraced with joy.

It was clear Father Hugh's education was more than his schooling. His life of faith nurtured by his family and friends, his childhood and teen years spent in Westfield, and his roots as a first-generation Irish American all contributed to his ability, as Pope Francis says, "to encounter, dialogue with, and accompany" so many people of different ages and backgrounds.

Father Hugh's desire to enter the ministry of parish life caused him to leave the Elms faculty and begin a journey of ultimately leading three parishes, including Holy Name Parish in Springfield, Massachusetts, from 1993 to 1999, and Our Lady of Blessed Sacrament Parish in Westfield, Massachusetts, from 1999 to 2004. But the focus of this essay will be Sacred Heart Parish in Springfield, Massachusetts, in which Father Hugh served as co-pastor with Father George Farland, from 1979 to 1989.

The perspective I bring to bear in this essay comes from my own lifelong attachment to Sacred Heart. As one who was born and grew up in the parish, and was educated in its schools, I have watched over the years as the parish continues to respond to the signs of the times. Father Hugh was assigned to reside in the parish when I was a teenager and appointed co-pastor when I was a young adult parishioner, a time described in sociology as the "coming of age" years, when people and events make an enduring impression on the thought and behavior of young people.

That was certainly the case in my life. The example of Father Hugh and Father George, the Sisters of Notre Dame de Namur with whom they collaborated, and the wonderful spirit of the parishioners as they shared their gifts, made the experience of Church a very positive one for me and helped me to discern my own vocation as a Sister of Notre Dame de Namur and to enter the congregation in 1981.

Researching and writing this essay has truly been a grace as it has allowed me to go back in time to a period that was so significant in many ways for many people. Focusing on the decade of the 1980s and his time as co-pastor with Father George allows us to recognize some themes that are important for the Church today. Let me locate that period of their ministry at Sacred Heart by sketching a brief history of this storied parish.

THE HISTORY OF SACRED HEART PARISH

Father Hugh appreciated history and had a deep regard for the history of Sacred Heart, of which he sometimes spoke in his homilies. In 1985, in one of his homilies, Father Hugh said, "Sacred Heart is a very interesting parish, almost 110 years old and going strong in its second century. The Church building has been the proud home for several generations of Catholics. . . . The parish has not only survived the flight to the suburbs, urban renewal, and population shifts—it has flourished as a still vibrant stable landmark in the city of Springfield." Father Hugh was aware of Sacred Heart's illustrious beginning in the nineteenth century and the particular challenges it, and other urban parishes, faced in the latter part of the twentieth century.

Sacred Heart's first pastor, Father James J. McDermott, was the first rector of Saint Michael's Cathedral, which had been built in 1861 on State Street, a more affluent side of the city of Springfield at that time. The large concentration of Irish immigrants located in the North End of the city called for the building of a church in that neighborhood a few years later. In fact, Sacred Heart Church can still be seen today from the front entrance of Union Station in Springfield, as it was first glimpsed by generations of European immigrants arriving in Springfield by train after their transatlantic voyage by boat to New York. The first glimpse of a Catholic Church by Irish immigrants in their new city may have caused them to recall their last glimpse of Saint Colman's Cathedral, which towers above the harbor of Cobh in County Cork, from which they had embarked.

Sacred Heart's early days closely follow the origin of the Diocese of Springfield, which was formed from the then-Diocese of Boston in 1870. Bishop O'Reilly announced the establishment of Sacred Heart Parish in 1872, and Father McDermott was named the first pastor of the new parish. The original Sacred Heart building was dedicated on Easter Sunday 1874, the cornerstone of the new church was laid in 1888, and the church completed in 1896.

Because of Father McDermott's belief in Catholic education, it was the first parish in the diocese to build the school before the church. The school opened in 1877, and the church was dedicated almost twenty years later, in 1896. In the intervening years, Mass was held in the school hall. In line with the Catholic Church's emphasis of that time on providing parochial education, Father McDermott famously said, "If I build my children a school, they will build me a church." And they did build a church—a magnificent Gothic Revival structure—at the corner of Chestnut and Linden (now Stafford) Streets.

Generations of parishioners of Sacred Heart have been justifiably proud of the soaring church edifice. The church was designed by James Murphy, an architect in Providence, Rhode Island. The original cost of the church was a hundred thousand dollars.

Father McDermott died in 1891, almost eighteen years after he came to Sacred Heart, and five years before the church was dedicated. Although the construction of the church was not complete, the funeral Mass for Father McDermott was held there. It was the first Mass held in the new church. Father McDermott was buried next to the church, where a monument was erected to him in 1920. The monument still stands.

Father McDermott was followed as pastor by Father Thomas Smythe. As the second pastor of the parish, Father Smythe served for thirty-six years, from 1891 to 1927. The third pastor was Father John F. Griffin, whose pastorate was brief, spanning from 1928 to 1930. Father Griffin was followed by Father Daniel H. McDermott (no relation to the first pastor), who served as pastor from 1931 to 1946. Father John D. Sullivan became pastor in 1946 and served until 1967. Father Sullivan was named monsignor in 1964. Father Donald F. Mullen served as pastor from 1967 until 1979. In 1979, Father Hugh F. Crean and Father George A. Farland were named co-pastors of Sacred Heart, serving together in those roles until 1989. Father George Farland (now Monsignor) had been assigned to Sacred Heart after his ordination in 1968. He has served as pastor of Sacred Heart since 1989.

THE CHURCH

Sacred Heart Church's grand exterior is rose-colored, rough-textured brownstone, which was quarried in East Longmeadow, Massachusetts. The magnificent interior is composed of twenty-seven stained-glass windows crafted in Munich, Germany, marble altars, carved oak pews which seat 1,600, sculpted Stations of the Cross, statuary, woodcarving, and an organ. Further discussion of the contemporary renovations of the church follows in the next section.

THE SISTERS OF NOTRE DAME DE NAMUR AND THE SCHOOLS

The Sisters of Notre Dame de Namur were invited by the first pastor, Father McDermott, to teach in Sacred Heart School. The same congregation of sisters was already teaching at Holy Name School in Chicopee, Massachusetts, the first parochial school in the Diocese of Springfield. The Sisters of Notre Dame de

Namur, an international congregation serving on five continents, was founded by Saint Julie Billiart in France in 1804. The Sisters arrived in the United States in 1840 and made their way to Chicopee in 1867.

Sacred Heart School was opened in September 1877 as an all-girls school. Seven sisters arrived in late August of that year to teach 330 girls. It was the first parochial school in the city. Boys were admitted to the school in 1908. The all-girls Sacred Heart High School was opened four years after the elementary school, in 1881.

In 1925, new grammar and high buildings were opened. In 1969, Sacred Heart High School and Holy Name High School in Chicopee were merged and became Notre Dame High School. The high school was closed in 1977 and the grammar school in 2002.

THE CO-PASTORATE OF FATHERS CREAN AND FARLAND

The co-pastorate of Father Hugh and Father George, from 1979 to 1989, was set against great ecclesial and societal change. They chose to co-pastor a unique urban parish that was located in a multicultural neighborhood that also crossed social class lines in a relatively small geographic space. Sacred Heart was made up of poor, working-class, middle-class, and upper-middle-class people.

The ministry of Fathers Hugh and George and their witness to the theological and pastoral vision of Vatican II gave stability, strength, hope, and joy in the midst of the myriad social forces that confronted urban parish life at that time. Some of those are recalled here as they illustrate the complex scene that energized and challenged ministry at that time.

ETHNIC DIVERSITY

While the Irish constituted a large number of the immigrants who came to the North End through the years, other ethnic groups also settled there. The diocese responded to the needs of immigrants by providing support via the construction of new parishes.

Two parishes were created from Sacred Heart—Our Lady of Hope in 1906 and All Souls in Brightwood in 1907. Our Lady of the Rosary Church was established on Franklin Street in 1917 to serve Polish-speaking Catholics.

In 1905, at the invitation of Bishop Beaven, Monsignor Paul Abi Saab came to Springfield to minister to the Lebanese Maronite people. For two years, he celebrated Mass at Sacred Heart Church for the Maronites. In 1907, he bought a parcel of land, and Saints Peter and Paul Lebanese Maronite Church was established on Liberty Street. It was renamed Saint Anthony of Padua Church in 1925.

The Spanish Apostolate was opened by the diocese in 1970, just a couple of blocks away from Sacred Heart. The Apostolate was located in a storefront on Chestnut Street, near the corner of Carew Street. Its mission was to respond to the needs of the people who had come from Puerto Rico, many of whom picked tobacco in the fields of northern Connecticut and settled in the North End.

Several Sisters of Notre Dame de Namur and Sisters of Providence were involved in part-time educational and health care ministry. Father George Farland, who had studied Spanish in Puerto Rico as part of his formation for priesthood, also was involved there. Father Mark Stelzer and I served as volunteer tutors in the summer of 1970 before our eighth-grade year at Sacred Heart School.

ELDERS

The construction of elderly high-rise apartment complexes constituted part of the transformation of the New North, the name given to the area near Sacred Heart in the late '60s, as old tenements were razed in order to build hundreds of units of housing for elders, as well as a new YMCA and Mercy Hospital. The housing complexes are Baystate Place, at the corner of Carew and Chestnut Streets; the Twin Towers (which later became the Tri-Towers), at Saab Court, off of Franklin Street; and the Hobby Club, on Chestnut Street. Saint Anthony's Church was razed during that time for the new buildings. Saab Court was named for its longtime pastor, Monsignor Michael Saab, who ministered in that area for fifty-three years, accompanying and then following his priest-uncle.

Sacred Heart reached out to the elders in those units throughout the years, providing pastoral care, First Friday Masses, and bus service to the church for

Mass on Sunday mornings. The parish also instituted an Over 60 Club, which offers monthly meetings, social events, and opportunities for travel, providing a sense of community. Students from Notre Dame High School were involved in several projects in ministry to the elders in the nearby high-rise apartment complexes. I can recall going with other students from the Young Christian Students (YCS) club, moderated by Sister Ellen Scanlon, SNDdeN, to visit some of the elders at their social events during Eastertime in the early 1970s.

URBAN UPHEAVAL

The 1960s had brought massive change to the North End of Springfield. Urban renewal tore through the parish as it demolished primarily two-family and three-family homes and tenements and displaced people who had lived there for generations. The demolition was followed by the construction of the 5.4-mile Interstate 291, linking the Massachusetts Turnpike, which runs east-west across the Commonwealth of Massachusetts, with Interstate 91, which runs north-south from Vermont, through Massachusetts, to Connecticut.

Longtime parishioners remember the dust from the demolition of homes and construction of the highway being everywhere. One Sister of Notre Dame said that they seemed to be "eating dust all the time." I remember, as a student in the school, the Sisters closing the windows to keep the dust out as they taught.

Parishioners remember being very upset because of the loss of a thriving working-class and diverse immigrant neighborhood with multiple businesses. Homes and streets were lost, causing some families like mine to relocate to the other side of the parish and others to move farther away. There was worry that urban renewal would destroy the parish and fear among the schoolchildren that the construction of the highway would take the church.

One longtime parishioner who remembers that time calls that period in the history of Springfield "urban removal." She says that many tears were shed as thousands of people were displaced when their homes were taken by eminent domain. She describes the renumeration they received for their homes as unjust. She says that some lined their pockets with gold while others lost all they had.

She recalls feeling sad as she often saw people crying during that time about the loss of their homes and neighborhood.

After the construction was completed, it was seen as paradoxical that the same highway that brought such grief by cutting through the parish, displacing residents and destroying homes, then served as a conduit through which people in other parts of the city and from multiple suburbs could have easier and quicker access to the church. The construction of the New North that razed buildings also opened up the local space allowing the church to serve as a majestic brownstone beacon of faith and hope, prominent in the urban landscape. Since 1968, people had been attracted to attend Mass at Sacred Heart from within and beyond the parish boundaries. The leadership of Fathers Hugh and George as co-pastors continued to draw people back to Sacred Heart from the suburbs to which they had moved and increasingly drew others as well.

CHURCH RENOVATION

There had been two major interior renovations of the church since the church's completion in 1896—in 1932 and in 1963. The magnificent Italian marble altar was installed in 1951. Plans for the third major interior renovation of the church commenced when Father Hugh and Father George were co-pastors, and the renovation was concluded in 1992. In terms of exterior work, the church was sandblasted in 1979, removing decades of soot, including the dust that had been raised in the building of Route 291. The sandblasting revealed a rose hue of the brownstone, surprising the younger parishioners and people in the area who grew up believing the brownstone was truly very dark. The sandblasting symbolized the freshness of a new beginning of the co-pastorate.

At that time, Father Leo E. O'Neil, the future bishop of Manchester, New Hampshire, composed the poem "From Route 291" about Sacred Heart's restored facade:

You boldly stand there on the corner
like some young girl blushing
at her own beauty.

Shame on you at your age
You should be fading into some quiet background
content with respectability, satisfied with reverence
not out there on the corner competing with younger
women for ohs and ahs of admiration.

More power to you grand old lady
flaunting your beauty and dazzling us
with elegance.

The sight of you on a spring morning with April greens
and cherry blossoms dancing at your side
lilts new songs and rose tints
the beginning of every day with the lure
of some beguiling promise that ageless beauty
does endure.

Stay always young Sacred Heart Church
for us who ride Route 291.

Always shouting to us about your beauty,
your newness, your incredible youth.

Be for us a sign of Church bursting forever
with spring rose tinting dawns and sunsets
with dreams fulfilled.

He loves His people and the glory of His dwelling
lifts up my soul.

The new model of co-pastoring allowed two priests to collaborate by sharing authority for the parish. There were only a couple of other examples of co-pastoring in the diocese at that time. In the case of Father Hugh and Father George, they also shared the preparation of the homily each week, with each delivering it in his own style but making similar points. The homilies were based in Scripture and grounded in God's love and mercy. A spirit of welcome, openness, and acceptance permeated the words and actions of the co-pastors. The witness of their own collaboration and teamwork, and their own deep friendship, strengthened the parish as it became a magnet for many who chose to worship there and experience God's love through the sacraments, particularly the celebration of the Eucharist, the preaching, and the community-diverse by age, ethnicity, income level, and background.

FATHER HUGH'S LEGACY

Father Hugh made choices in his life and ministry that continue to provide inspiration. He chose to place himself within parish life and be touched by its daily and very human demands. Indeed, in his first weekend homily as co-pastor of Sacred Heart, he stated that he believed it was the dream of every diocesan priest to one day have a parish that he could serve. He called service at Sacred Heart "a sacred trust." He knew Sacred Heart Parish well since he lived in its rectory for a total of nineteen years—while he taught at the Elms, served as co-pastor, and when he was Diocesan Vicar for Priests and Director of Clergy Personnel (1989–1992).

At the same time, he did not allow his deep sense of service to the parish to overwhelm his broad vision of ministry and Church. The parish became the primary, but not the only, locus where his vision was articulated and lived. Sacred Heart Parish was his anchor and his community, no matter how or where he shared his gifts. Father Hugh also gave faithful service to the diocese through multiple appointments to boards and committees and traveled frequently to give retreats to priests.

For years, Father Hugh gave public lectures at the Elms sharing the fruits of Vatican II, giving multiple lectures on Scripture to Sisters and laypersons. His lectures drew rapt audiences who wished to deepen their knowledge and avail themselves of his theological expertise. One laywoman, remembering those lectures and Father Hugh's insights into the Gospel, recalled that they deepened her faith, as they were scripturally based and theologically rich.

Father George Farland, delivering the homily at the Mass at Sacred Heart celebrating the twenty-fifth anniversary of Father Hugh's ordination to the priesthood, said, "I have . . . as others have, learned much from Hugh Crean, not only from his spoken word but also by his life lived. . . . It is my opinion that in the competitive secular society he would be second-to-none. But twenty-five years ago, Hugh in faith chose another road—a road less traveled. He committed himself to the priesthood of Jesus Christ and in humility has brought the message of forgiveness, hope, healing, and the promise of eternal life to God's people."

Father George's reference in his homily to learning from Father Hugh's "spoken word" and "his life lived" point to that rare combination that constitutes his enduring legacy—the breadth of his cosmopolitan vision and the depth of his parochial ministry, and how he wove the two with grace.

In a talk he delivered in the 1980s, Father Hugh broke open his broad vision of Church ministry:

> The world press made a very serious mistake when all the newspapers, radio, and TV reports announced that Vatican Council II had ended. In reality, it was just beginning. We are now living in this new era which is both a time of great hope and confidence, youthful vitality and regeneration, and a time of upheaval and turmoil. But possibly the times in which we live as Church are disclosing a phenomenon of very deep significance for the present and the future—and that is the gradual emergence of a deep authentic ministry of the layperson, not to replace or supplant the religious and clergy but to share in that gift and responsibility.
>
> The whole Church is in ministry. According to the New Testament, it is not a question of *whether* we are called to ministry but of *how* we are called. The pattern in the past has often been to depend on the clergy and religious alone. The clergy and religious have a vocation within the Church without question, but so do the laypersons have vocations to the Church because the Church is

> all of us. And so, we establish that the Church is inclusive of lay ministers as well as clergy.
>
> Since the end of Vatican II, we have seen in the Church an unprecedented reform of structures. The whole style of leadership has undergone or is undergoing change. . . . Left behind in all of this, at least to some extent, are most of the people in the pews. Many are confused, disappointed; some are in disagreement and some are there anxious and eager to be of service to the Church, but they don't know how. It is now the average people in the pews who need renewal, who need to be brought into personal contact with Christ and the Church, who need to be given real, human, significant contact with the parish community of which they are a part.
>
> Two cautions:
> It will take a long time (not a parish mission).
> It cannot be mandated from above but must rise out of the felt needs of the people in the pew.
>
> It requires a serious rethinking of what is the meaning of the Church.

Father Hugh's broad vision of Vatican II ministry and the meaning of the Church was made real in his daily encounters with the people of the parish and their hopes and fears. The following three excerpts of talks he gave in the parish illustrate his ability to listen to and learn from the members of his parish family and to know and affirm the journey he shared with them. The talks were given at an elementary school graduation as a homily about elders in the parish and as a eulogy for a Sister of Notre Dame de Namur.

As co-pastor, Father Hugh delivered a talk at the graduation of the eighth-grade class of Sacred Heart School in 1988, in which he said, "I praise our school which believes in God—in the equality of boys and girls, black and white and brown, rich and poor—all equal before God. . . . I want to praise our children who through the years and even today learn to be kind and tolerant, to love God and people, to care about each other and love their fellow men and women."

In a eulogy for Sister Thomasine O'Connor, SNDdeN, who had been part of the pastoral team with Father Hugh and Father George and who died of cancer in her late sixties after a short period of illness, Father Hugh said:

> I compare her life and ministry to that of Christ Himself.
>
> Like Jesus, who spent 30 years in the background listening, observing, and reflecting in silence, Thomasine lived a quiet life in the kitchen at Emmanuel College in Boston. Like Jesus, who eventually burst into the spotlight during his years of public ministry, Thomasine burst into the spotlight in parish ministry, doing the very same things Jesus did during his years of public ministry. In imitation of Jesus, Thomasine taught and healed. She gave comfort to the sick and grieved with the mourning. She laughed and cried with the rich and the poor. In recent months, she bore the Cross which a cancer diagnosis brings.
>
> Everyone here knows that, like Jesus, Thomasine was at home with all kinds of people. She could be seen in the downtown soup kitchen or in the homes of the rich. She brought God's peace to the elderly whenever she brought the Eucharist to their homes or apartments. Thomasine brought laughter to Over 60 Club meetings, trips, and parties. She organized a food fund for the poor and Thanksgiving dinners for the needy. She brought flowers to nursing homes.
>
> At Sacred Heart, Thomasine taught kindergarten and supervised religious education classes. She was especially proud of each year's First Communion class. She loved Baptism preparation classes and conducted them with a special grace. Nervous brides met her for wedding rehearsals and usually left with a smile on their faces and appreciation in their hearts. Thomasine sold raffle tickets anywhere and everywhere for the benefit of the parish or some worthy organization like

> the Hibernians. She had an energy and purpose that was boundless. She was playful and completely without guile or pretense.

In a homily on the Gospel of the widow's mite, Father Hugh preached, "Support for Sacred Heart has often come from many people consistently making their contribution without show or fanfare week after week. I believe today's gospel is about these people. Here at Sacred Heart, we have many widows, widowers, and people of all ages who give from their want, and we are grateful. This parish will continue. Many more babies will be baptized, children educated, and, with God's help, a growing generation of young people who, like their parents, will believe in sacrifice for their Church. The widow of the Gospel will still live, and love, and serve here at Sacred Heart."

Father Hugh will have the last word in this essay. We have seen his extraordinary ability to bring the worlds of the Universal Church together with the local Church, and we have heard his stirring call for lay involvement rooted in Vatican II that anticipated Pope Francis's vision of synodality, or ways of becoming a Church characterized by participation, communion, and mission.

Yet, in the introduction he intended for this collection of his homilies and talks, we read an admonition to Church leaders and preachers that is particularly prescient for the Church today. In that introduction, Father Hugh describes his vision of what Church leaders and preachers are called to be: "We are not judges but ministers of God's love and patience . . . we are bridge builders, faith interpreters, and ambassadors of God's kindness."

And so Father Hugh was.

Shadow and Light, Doubt and Faith: Signs of the Sacred

PETER A. DEPERGOLA II, PHD

> "Lord, I believe; help my unbelief!" (Mark 9:24) is a contradiction, seemingly, for if he believes, if he trusts, how is it that he beseeches the Lord to help his lack of trust? Nevertheless, it is the contradiction that gives to the heart's cry of the father of the demoniac its most profound human value. His faith is a faith that is based upon uncertainty. Because he believes—that is to say, because he wishes to believe—he asks the Lord to help his belief, his doubt that such a cure can happen. Of such kind is human faith—a faith based upon doubt.
>
> —Hugh F. Crean, homily, "Shadow and Light, Doubt and Faith: Signs of the Sacred Within"

INTRODUCTION

In 1973, under the direction of the distinguished Belgian Jesuit and dogmatic theologian Piet Fransen (1913–1983), Father Hugh F. Crean (1937–2015) earned his Doctor of Philosophy and Doctor of Sacred Theology degrees from the Catholic University of Louvain. The subject of Crean's dissertation was the relationship between doubt and faith in the theology of the German American existentialist philosopher and Lutheran Protestant theologian Paul Tillich (1886–1965). In one of the last recorded statements of his life, Tillich reflected on his vocation as shepherding "those people who are in doubt or estrangement or opposition to anything ecclesiastical and religious, including Christianity. My work is with those who ask questions, and for them I am here." Mirroring his scholastic muse, Crean, too, would dedicate his academic and pastoral life to sharing the light of faith with those who lived in the shadow of doubt. It is against this backdrop that Crean's theological method is best understood.

For Crean, Tillich's appreciation and presupposition of Christian history enabled him to perceptively understand his own times and minister to the needs of his contemporaries. Like Tillich, Crean himself was a questioner, an inquisitive mind that felt most alive in the company of kindred spirits on the journey from doubt to analysis, and from analysis to faith. For those in the shadow of doubt, Tillich's message of faith was one Crean knew well and exercised in his own ministry. Crean found in Tillich's theological method many notes of synchronicity, including Tillich's contention that in order to heal others with faith, faith itself required healing. Due to its commonplace misuse, Tillich argued, "the only way of dealing with the problem [of the definition of 'faith'] is to try to reinterpret the word and remove the confusing and distorting connotations, some of which are the heritage of centuries." For Tillich, the full meaning of faith is inextricably bound up with doubt, and thus an authentic interpretation of faith must include a careful analysis of the human experience of doubt.

This essay attempts to unveil and clarify the subject of Crean's greatest academic preoccupation: Tillich's analysis of the interconnection between doubt and faith, with special attention paid to the positive role that doubt plays in the development of faith. To that end, it moves in four parts. First, it examines the phenomenology of doubt, including a specific analysis of the role of existentialism in Tillich's theology. Second, it addresses the dialectic of doubt and faith, including a specific analysis of doubt as the intellectual process by which faith is deepened. Third, it explores anxiety as the opportunity for grace, including a specific analysis of the contributions of Tillich's great contemporary, the German phenomenologist-philosopher Martin Heidegger (1889–1976). Fourth, it considers the christening of anxiety and doubt through faith by grace, including a specific analysis of the theological parallels between Heidegger and Tillich on the subject of ultimate concern. The essay concludes by sketching the implications of Tillich's theology of faith on contemporary culture, especially as it pertains to those to whom Crean passionately ministered during life's moments of severest doubt: the critically ill.

THE PHENOMENOLOGY OF DOUBT

According to Tillich, the paralyzing anxiety of doubt characterizes the milieu in which humanity is presently situated. As the unintended fixation of our time, we struggle to identify our spiritual center, and the world of objects we have created has subsumed us and our ability to live meaningful lives in the process. As Tillich writes, "the question arising out of this experience is not . . . the question of a merciful God and the forgiveness of sins; nor is it . . . the question of finitude, of death and error; nor is it the question of the personal religious life or of the Christianization of culture and society. It is a question of a reality in which the self-estrangement of our existence is overcome, a reality of reconciliation and reunion, of creativity, meaning, and hope." In this situation—one in which almost all traditional values and forms of life are disintegrating—humanity is driven to the abyss of complete meaninglessness. As a result, we are left aimless and desperate to identify the purpose and meaning of life itself, and so find ourselves in a maze of unresolved questions and inescapable tensions.

The philosophical lens through which Tillich approaches doubt is thoroughly existentialist. His writings lean heavily on the literary works of Jean-Paul Sartre (1905–1980), T. S. Eliot (1888–1965), Franz Kafka (1883–1924), W. H. Auden (1907–1973), Albert Camus (1913–1960), Arthur Miller (1915–2005), and Tennessee Williams (1911–1983), each of whom endeavored to pinpoint the phenomenology of meaninglessness. In the philosophical works of Heidegger, Karl Jaspers (1883–1969), Sartre, and Gabriel Marcel (1889–1973), Tillich found what he believed to be the strongest theoretical formulation of the problem of humanity's ceaseless battle with meaninglessness. As for his own specific analysis, Tillich's sermons overflow with echoes of existentialist thought as it pertains to the human thirst for meaning. His project is to confront humanity with the reality of its own finitude and alienation by focusing on the situations that most acutely reveal it: anguish, loneliness, and insecurity. It is for this reason that Tillich boldly claims that the cardinal role of the minister is to place the faithful before themselves so that they can—perhaps for the first time—peel back the *velum* of self-deception and finally face their precarious state.

To describe humanity's earthly lot, Tillich argues that "doubt, and not servitude, is [the fundamental element] of our human situation." If we take seriously the call to critically analyze our own character, Tillich writes, we can accurately summarize our state as an autonomous people who have become insecure in our autonomy. A symptom of this insecurity is that we no longer possess a worldview based on the embodied experience of God, the world, and ourselves. We no longer possess a self-rule by which we are self-assured and creative. Instead, we are possessed by an autonomy that leaves us disturbed, frustrated, and in despair. To catalogue the language employed by Tillich to describe the human condition is to paint a joyless and pessimistic picture. Tillich holds no punches as he describes his fellow human beings as trapped in meaninglessness, emptiness, helplessness, uncertainty, insecurity, frustration, and doubt. Yet he uses this language to describe the cracks in humanity that begin the healing journey toward the dawning light of Christ. Due to the revelation-salvation dimension of our lives, humanity is not perpetually bound to meaninglessness. However, the persistent experience of meaninglessness, even in light of this divine dimension, highlights the reality of our inability for self-salvation. Tillich holds out two alternatives for humanity: "despair, which is the certainty of eternal destruction[,] or faith, which is the certainty of eternal salvation."

THE DIALECTIC OF DOUBT AND FAITH

To understand the mechanism by which humanity moves from despair to faith, it is important to review the dialectic shared between them. Tillich contends that the first step in solving the problem of doubt is to admit that the very question cannot ultimately be answered. After all, God cannot be reached or controlled by the intellectual or moral work of his creation. In Tillich's words, "just as you are justified as a sinner . . . so in the state of doubt you are in the status of truth. And if all this comes together and you are desperate about the meaning of life, the seriousness of your despair is the expression of the meaning in which you are still living." Asserted here is the fact that humanity, in our finiteness and contingency, faces life without problems solved and questions answered, and yet "in every doubt the formal affirmation of truth as truth is presupposed." That is, while we seek to overcome our doubt by every possible means, the intensity of our quest and search for truth and meaning is heightened, and thus our doubt is as dynamic as our faith.

For Tillich, radical doubt is not simply an intellectual malfunction in need of healing; it is a deep religious experience that has the potential for spiritual regeneration. The doubter walks the line between despair and hope, yet it is precisely on this line that the purpose and meaning of existence can be found. To be sure, the answer to radical doubt "must accept, as its precondition, the state of meaninglessness." In order to seek an answer to the situation in which we find ourselves, we must first accept that situation—not in a spirit of resignation to an unchangeable state of affairs but in the sense that we realistically perceive our existential lot and face it head-on. Tillich maintains that to accept the situation of doubt paradoxically requires faith: "The act of accepting meaninglessness is in itself a meaningful act. It is an act of faith." To Tillich's mind, accepting doubt as part and parcel of human existence is a courageous act of faith by which one discovers meaning and truth. For the one who is seized by God, doubt becomes a means by which to penetrate the depths of one's own being and of all being. Thus, doubt undercuts "the untested assumptions on which our lives are built. . . . And then it happens that those who live in serious doubt . . . discover that dimension that leads to the ultimate by which they have been arrested. And they realize that hidden in the seriousness of their doubt was the truth."

Tillich insists that the quality, or "seriousness," of the doubt in question is a barometer by which the depth of its preconditional faith and the intensity of its corresponding search for truth and meaning is measured. The individual who is arrested by God is someone in the state of doubt, yet the doubt is not an obstacle but a *via* to the deepening realization of truth and meaning. Through doubt, humanity is stripped of our unexamined presuppositions, and, by considering the most important matters of consequence in our lives—that is, by articulating our "ultimate concern"—we discover truth hidden in the solemn effort to believe. The breakthrough of grace and subsequent theological certitude is prepared by this experience of doubt. To be sure, we do not set the breakthrough in motion, but through God's initiative, we are grasped, arrested, and held by his sovereign power. When discussing Saint Paul's First Letter to the Corinthians, during which the apostle exhorts the community to remain watchful, faithful, courageous, and strong (1 Cor. 16:13), Tillich explains that standing firm in faith is not a mere adherence to a set of beliefs but a stance in honesty whereby doubt and unbelief are taken seriously and without restriction. In so doing, Tillich says, we discover and become aware of a real faith that we can claim as our own.

In his analysis of the paradoxical dialectic between doubt and faith, Tillich rejects the intellectualistic overtone of adherence to a set of propositions and reemphasizes the presence of doubt in the risk of faith, which embraces and integrates doubt into its subsequent movements. Here, doubt is understood not simply as a negative evil—a *privatio boni*—but an experience that deepens and enriches the understanding and meaning of one's faith. To take one's doubt seriously, Tilich believes, is to be inevitably led to faith. This sentiment is expressed in his sermon "On Healing," where he remarks that "faith . . . does not mean belief in assertions for which there is no evidence. . . . Faith means being grasped by a power that is greater than we are, a power that shakes us and turns us, and transforms us and heals us. Surrender to this power of faith." Tillich's emphasis is on God's action in seizing humanity, which through his power is transformed and healed. In such circumstances, our doubt is overcome but not eradicated, and healed precisely at the moment it is integrated. We, for our part, surrender to God's power in "an acceptance of an acceptance."

According to Tillich, as humanity faces the abyss of meaninglessness, there is at least one truth that emerges with clarity: we do not possess the truth. In other words, our finite existence is far from being the self-sufficient state that we often believe it to be. Through the experience of radical doubt in the acknowledgment of our own finitude, humanity is on the threshold of despair. At that moment, a completely new meaning appears: doubt has stripped away self-sufficiency and self-salvation, and we—on the brink of despair—understand with the totality of our being that human existence has its source and summit in something other than ourselves. This is not a discovery of a partial truth or meaning but the experience of being grasped by something transcendent. Just as there is doubt existing in all authentic faith, so too is there faith existing in all serious doubt. For Tillich, there is no faith without an intrinsic "in spite of" and the courageous affirmation of oneself in the state of ultimate concern. This doubt is not a denial of faith per se but something structurally present in the act of faith that "was always and will always be present." In the final analysis, "faith is the courage that conquers doubt, not by removing it, but by taking it as an element into itself. . . . The element of doubt, conquered in faith, is never completely lacking in any serious affirmation of God."

THE CHRISTENING OF ANXIETY THROUGH FAITH BY GRACE

Arguably the greatest of Crean's scholarly contributions to the analysis of Tillich on doubt as a structural element of faith is the innovative and unexpected parallels he draws between Tillich and Heidegger. While Tillich does not explicitly acknowledge Heidegger by name in his work, the similarities between the two thinkers are significant. It was through Heidegger that Tillich was first introduced to twentieth-century existentialism, yet there are relatively few references to Heidegger's philosophy in Tillich's three-volume *Systematic Theology,* and even fewer elsewhere. Nevertheless, Crean's insight that Heidegger's analysis of anxiety may be a useful mechanism by which to unlock Tillich's analysis of doubt is one that merits close attention. The negativity commonly attributed to the experience of anxiety, for Heidegger, and the negativity commonly attributed to the experience of doubt, for Tillich, are recast in positive light in the construction of their respective philosophical and theological approaches. For Heidegger and Tillich, anxiety and doubt remain negative elements of humanity's experience, but they take on positive value and function in unexpected ways. Before examining the theoretical similarities between Heidegger on anxiety and Tillich on doubt, it is necessary, first, to become familiar with Heidegger's phenomenology of anxiety and its place within the ontology of human experience.

For Heidegger, humanity's quest for meaning is unique insofar as it questions the state of being itself. This is precisely the element of consciousness that privileges us, sets us apart, and distinguishes us from all other sentient beings. Heidegger uses a very specific term for this search, not simply for contextual meaning but for being itself: *Dasein,* or "there-being." Heidegger holds that truth and meaning are filtered through the subjectivity of judgment by what he terms "mood." Being is given to humanity only in understanding, and the understanding subject always possesses some mood (*gestimmt-ist*). This mood is not simply a subjective knowledge but an awareness that is spontaneous and unreflective; it measures "how one is and how one is faring" (*wie einem ist und wird*). Thus understood, mood is an ontological disposition that is cumbersomely but accurately described by the Jesuit philosopher William Richardson as "the already-having-found-itself-there-ness of there-being." Mood, then, is a primordial mode of being for *Dasein* in which *Dasein* is disclosed to itself prior to all cognition and volition, is beyond the range of disclosure, and colors the relationship of *Dasein* with all other beings and objects.

In *Being and Time,* Heidegger asks whether *Dasein* possesses an understanding state of mind, or mood, in which *Dasein* has been disclosed to itself in some distinctive way. He answers that *Dasein* is disclosed in a specific way through the experience of *Angst,* or "anxiety." This disclosure takes place inasmuch as *Angst* brings *Dasein* before itself as "being in the world," as the coming to pass of transcendence. Hence, *Angst* is the comprehensive disposition by which *Dasein* is, in its unity, disclosed to itself. For Heidegger, the meaninglessness of other objects or beings in the world, the futility of participation in life as it is disclosed here and now, and the terminal indefiniteness of everything is the source of humanity's anxiety. This anxiety differs from fear insofar as fear is localized and identifiable whereas anxiety is epidemic and indefinite.

It is ultimately about nonbeing that *Dasein* is anxious, yet this nonbeing is grounded, paradoxically, in something. According to Heidegger, the something in which nonbeing is grounded is the world itself. Through anxiety, the world *qua* world is exposed, but this process does not begin in understanding and end in anxiety but rather begins in anxiety and ends in understanding. That is, through the awareness of the meaning of nothingness, it is possible to be led to the meaning of being. In this sense, *Angst* prepares and disposes *Dasein* to understand that there exists something over and against the terror of awareness that first leads it into being.

Heidegger's identification of transcendence to being and its movement in relation to nonbeing is critical, Crean argues, to understanding the similarities it shares with Tillich's conception of doubt. For Heidegger, the positive actualization process of transcendence—which is the solitary and elusive project of *Dasein*—takes place through a courageous encounter with nonbeing. Only by entering the abyss of nothingness does one push up against the somethingness of being.

The negativity of *Angst* and its ensuing dread is the cost of transcendence insofar as transcendence is accomplished exclusively by the painful experience of being colliding with nonbeing. In *Angst*, the void of nonbeing opens up within its being. That is, the negative and positive interpenetrate one another in the dynamic process that envelops *Dasein*. The negative is represented by the painful experience of abandonment that characterizes *Angst*, and *Angst* implies *Dasein*'s care for itself. *Angst* does not abolish care but rather serves as its foundation by forcing *Dasein* to withdraw from the world only to let it return, albeit safeguarded against the possibility of losing itself in the contentment and satisfaction of the world alone. Heidegger's claim here is that to be thrust into nonbeing is the way to transcendence: the negative perdurance of *Angst* is the other side of the positive process of becoming through transcendence. Thus understood, *Angst* is not merely a negative factor in the finitude of human existence but the dispositional occasion for the positive expression of care. Indeed, it is *Angst* endured through courage that produces possibility.

When Tillich's phenomenology of doubt is juxtaposed with Heidegger's metaphysics of *Angst*, an unmistakable affinity between the two thinkers emerges within their common analysis of the paradox of positivity in negativity. For Heidegger, *Angst* is positive insofar as it disposes humanity for the discovery of being. For Tillich, doubt is positive insofar as it disposes humanity for a new awareness or discovery of God. For both thinkers, the encounter with nonbeing is equal parts threat and possibility, and it is precisely for this reason that it enables us to discover transcendence. The indispensable companion to *Angst* and doubt is courage, which is self-affirmation of being in the face of nonbeing. Both Heidegger and Tillich stress the importance of this self-affirmation, but not to such an extent as to devalue *Angst* or doubt or rob them of their seriousness. Rather, self-affirmation, properly understood, embraces *Angst* and doubt as first movements in the process of discovery. To be sure, echoes of Tillich's intellectual kinship with Heidegger are discernible in various places in his works, yet it would be a mistake to equate Heidegger with Tillich. Of course, what Heidegger sees Tillich also observes, but the latter through the lens of a believer—a Christian theologian and also a philosopher. Despite their diverging starting points and personal convictions, Crean contends strongly that Heidegger's philosophy of *Angst* vividly illustrates the positive dimension and function of doubt in Tillich's theology of faith.

According to Crean, the most substantive, fundamental, and significant reason for viewing doubt positively is that it marks the dispositional occasion for the breakthrough of grace. Tillich vehemently rejects the possibility of humanity's action being responsible for this breakthrough by the act of doubt or through any other action. Rather, for Tillich, the source of God's grace is absolutely gratuitous and sovereign. While humanity cannot cause grace per se, doubt produces a new receptivity for grace that the doubter has acquired. Confronted with our inability to know God in toto, we doubt and are subsequently grasped, in our doubting, by ultimate concern itself. The doubt is positive insofar as it serves as the mechanism by which grace, truth, and meaning infiltrate the soul. Tillich hastens to clarify that this is only the case if one also doubts one's doubt—that is, if the doubter does not permit doubt to become another form of possession. Doubt safeguards faith from the demonic due to its constant challenge to the doubter. In this way, it is the explicit corrective to faith, preventing it from becoming a creaturely possession rather than a divine process. The process of faith, then, is one that begins with a certainty of faith based on the radical awareness of the unconditional God.

CONCLUSION

Beyond Crean's theological engrossment in the relationship between doubt and faith, his personal interest in the subject arose from years of pastoral ministry. Through numerous encounters with youth groups, college students, adult converts, and elderly cradle Catholics, he was confronted constantly by the reality that radical existential doubt is part and parcel of human experience. Crean recounts the sense of unworthiness, estrangement, and despair that characterized many individuals to whom he ministered and that the question of faith—of reasons to believe—loomed largest of all. It was Tillich's claim that faith was not a thing to be had but a search—a journey amid the shadow of doubt—that propelled Crean to focus his ministry on comforting those who realize anew, in nearly every season of life, that faith and doubt must be in creative tension in order to bear fruit.

A careful reading of Crean yields still another rich yet heretofore unarticulated element of his scholarship: the implied vision of hope as the abiding and malleable bridge from doubt to faith, from faith to expectation, and from expectation to desire. As the theological virtue by which humanity desires the kingdom of heaven and eternal life as our happiness—placing our trust in Christ's promises and relying not on our own strength—hope is the wellspring of courage to persevere in times of profound doubt. Thus understood, hope rescues us from the discouragement induced by doubt, sustains us in faith during times of seeming abandonment, and develops us in love and expectation of eternal beatitude. Christian hope takes up and fulfills the hope of the chosen people, which has its origins and model par excellence in the hope of Abraham, who, "hoping against hope" (Rom. 4:18), believed in the promises of God and was purified by the test of his sacrifice. Such hope is perhaps nowhere more fragile than in the lives of those to whom Crean often ministered during his life: the critically ill.

As Crean witnessed firsthand when ministering to parishioners living with serious illnesses, clinicians often struggle with imparting hope in providing patient care, especially for those at the end of life. Although clinicians intuitively appreciate the therapeutic benefits of hope, concern about discouraging hope is a common reason for delaying important conversations about poor prognoses. Conversely, clinicians are equally concerned when patients have unrealistic hope for a cure or a longer life and thus feel compelled to correct patients' hope to enable more empirically informed decisions. Notwithstanding these seemingly competing obligations, possessing hope—which is neither dichotomous nor static but complex, continuous, and contextual—is psychologically beneficial. A 2002 report indicated that more than fifty studies suggested that hope was associated with improved physical and mental health, relationships, functional status, and coping. In a recent systematic review of hope-fostering interventions among approximately 3,300 patients in thirty-five studies, promoting hope was associated with improved patient-reported meaning and purpose and decreased symptoms of depression. In their journey from doubt to faith, hope promotes in patients a sense of control, forward momentum, and incentive in an otherwise uncontrollable, stagnant, and paralyzing experience.

In light of growing evidence that religiosity is inversely associated with death anxiety and that high levels of unmet spiritual need are associated with lower levels of satisfaction and perception of health care quality, the role of clinicians—like the role of pastoral ministers—is not to prioritize a single likely or unlikely hope but to help patients recognize and diversify the breadth of their hope. In time, this effort allows patients to psychologically adjust, identify goal-concordant decisions, and more successfully navigate their illness. This is what Crean deduced from Tillich, and hence what we can deduce from Crean: humanity, both parishioners and patients alike, must be allowed to experience the sadness and fear of doubt without being so overwhelmed that they cannot simultaneously continue to live out a hope guided by faith. Discouraging hope, like discouraging doubt, is rarely constructive, and thus it is incumbent on courageous leaders, whether chaplains or clinicians, to recognize differences between tangible hope for finding meaning in the moment and more nebulous desires for an unlikely future. This delicate endeavor necessitates comfort with the anxiety of uncertain ideas, entails readiness to navigate negative emotions, and demands continued conversation and willingness to both change direction and move forward without knowing what is coming.

Crean intimately understood that accepting and coping with critical illness does not happen quickly, and that walking in hope from doubt to faith (2 Cor. 5:7) requires steadfast patience. Rather than being concerned that hope, like faith, is either so fragile that it can be lost, or so powerful that it can overwhelm decision making, Crean's clarion call to clinicians is that hope, like doubt, is protective, if not fundamentally necessary for managing critical illness.

Grounded in Tillich's analysis of doubt as a means by which humanity is opened to the possibility of faith by grace, Crean challenges all of us not to expel doubt or wish away the problems of uncertainty and meaninglessness but to look to the example of Jesus of Nazareth, who endured the same experiences and yet was not overcome by them. By the power of Christ, then, we can believe in the unlikely while simultaneously accepting the inevitable. To take Crean's instruction on the tumultuous journey from doubt to faith is to finally be able to say, with Saint Paul, that we are a people saved in hope (Rom. 8:24).

REFERENCES

Astrow, Alan B., Gary Kwok, Rashmi K. Sharma, Nelli Fromer, and Daniel P. Sulmasy. "Spiritual Needs and Perception of Quality of Care and Satisfaction with Care in Hematology/Medical Oncology Patients: A Multicultural Assessment." *Journal of Pain and Symptom Management* 55, no. 1 (2018): 56–64.e1.

Catechism of the Catholic Church. 2nd ed. Citta del Vaticano: Libreria Editrice Vaticana, 1997.

Crean, Hugh F. "Faith and Doubt in the Theology of Paul Tillich." *Bijdragen: Tijdschrift Voor Filosofie en Theologie* 36, no. 2 (1975): 145–64.

Folkman, Susan. "Stress, Coping, and Hope." *Psycho-Oncology* 19, no. 9 (2010): 901–8.

Heidegger, Martin. *Being and Time,* translated by John Macquarrie and Edward Robinson. Oxford: Basil Blackwell, 1967.

Henrie, James, and Julie Hicks Patrick. "Religiousness, Religious Doubt, and Death Anxiety." *International Journal of Aging and Human Development* 78, no. 3 (2014): 203–27.

Jackson, Vicki A., Juliet Jacobsen, Joseph A. Greer, William F. Pirl, Jennifer S. Temel, and Anthony L. Back. "The Cultivation of Prognostic Awareness Through the Provision of Early Palliative Care in the Ambulatory Setting: A Communication Guide." *Journal of Palliative Medicine* 16, no. 8 (2013): 894–900.

Richardson, William J. *Heidegger: Through Phenomenology to Thought.* The Hague: Martinus Nijhoff, 1967.

Rosenberg, Abby, Robert M. Arnold, and Yael Schenker. "Holding Hope for Patients with Serious Illness." *Journal of the American Medical Association* 326, no. 13 (2021): 1259–60.

Salamanca-Balen, Natalia, Thomas V. Merluzzi, and Man Chen. "The Effectiveness of Hope-Fostering Interventions in Palliative Care: A Systematic Review and Meta-Analysis." *Palliative Medicine* 35, no. 4 (2021): 710–28.

Snyder, C. R., Kevin L. Rand, Elisa A. King, David B. Feldman, and Julia T. Woodward. "'False' Hope." *Journal of Clinical Psychiatry* 58, no. 9 (2002): 1003–22.

Tillich, Paul. *Dynamics of Faith.* New York: Harper & Row, 1958.

Tillich, Paul. "Estrangement and Reconciliation in Modern Thought." *The Review of Religion* IX (1944): 5–19.

Tillich, Paul. *On the Boundary: An Autobiographical Sketch.* New York: Charles Scribner's Sons, 1966.

Tillich, Paul. *Systematic Theology,* Vols. 1–3. London: James Nisbet and Company, 1968.

Tillich, Paul. *The Courage to Be.* New Haven, CT: Yale University Press, 1952.

Tillich, Paul. *The Eternal Now.* New York: Charles Scribner's Sons, 1963.

Tillich, Paul. *The New Being.* New York: Charles Scribner's Sons, 1955.

Tillich, Paul. *The Protestant Era,* translated by James Luther Adams. Chicago: University of Chicago Press, 1957.

Tillich, Paul. *The Shaking of the Foundations.* New York: Charles Scribner's Sons, 1948.

Tillich, Paul. *Ultimate Concern: Tillich in Dialogue,* edited by D. Mackenzie Brown. New York: Harper & Row, 1965.

Priesthood: A Sacrament of Friendship

MARK S. STELZER, STD

INTRODUCTION

In many ways, 1962 was a memorable year for Catholics living in the United States. The first session of the Second Vatican Council, which introduced widespread changes in the Church, opened in Rome in October of that year. As David O'Brien reminds us in his essay, John F. Kennedy, who had been elected in 1960 as the country's first Catholic president, continued to win the hearts of many Americans, especially those of Irish Catholic descent.

In 1962, the United States and Soviet Union were on the brink of war following the discovery of Soviet missile bases on beaches surrounding the Bay of Pigs. At the same time, the United States was slowly escalating its involvement in Vietnam. On the domestic front, civil rights activists were winning hard-earned victories against segregationists while *West Side Story* continued to challenge cultural mores and prejudices related to cultural assimilation and belonging. John Glenn became the first American to orbit the earth.

During these and other major events in the life of the Church and wider society, Hugh Francis Crean was ordained a priest on May 26, 1962. Ordained with him that day at Saint Michael's Cathedral in Springfield, Massachusetts, were Rene Coté, Rudolph Guillemette, Raymond O'Sullivan, and Richard Sniezyk. Following the customary two-week vacation afforded newly ordained priests, Hugh began his first assignment as a curate, or associate pastor, at Saint Michael's Parish in East Longmeadow, Massachusetts.

Hugh spoke frequently and with great fondness of the seven years (1962–1969) he spent in East Longmeadow. In those years, East Longmeadow was a rapidly growing New England town populated by young families living in newly constructed Kay Vee homes, all built by the same developer in almost identical style. The seven-hundred-plus school-age children registered in the parish's faith formation program were what we now call "baby boomers."

As was the custom in most parishes in that era, the parish's sixty-five-year-old pastor, Father John Wolohan, entrusted almost all youth activities to his twenty-five-year-old associate.[107]

Although Hugh spent much of his time as an associate pastor recruiting volunteers and organizing catechetical and social activities for school-age children, he also devoted considerable time and energy to planning and executing adult education programs intended to introduce parishioners to the reforms of the Second Vatican Council. In many ways a revolutionary council, Vatican II (1962–1965) effected major liturgical changes, including the introduction of the Mass in the vernacular, or language of the people. Vatican II also encouraged Catholics to rethink Church systems and structures. Even more fundamentally, Vatican II argued for a process of Church reform guided by the principles of *ressourcement* and *aggiornamento.*[108]

Even though the changes being proposed by Vatican II overwhelmed many Catholics, Hugh's four years at Saint Mary's Seminary in Baltimore (1958–1962) had, to no small degree, prepared him for the impending winds of change that impacted parishes like Saint Michael's. At Saint Mary's Seminary, Hugh had been exposed to the thought of influential contributors to the Council such as Yves Congar and Henri de Lubac.[109] He and his seminary classmates had carefully followed the progress of the preparatory sessions leading up to Vatican II. As a result, Hugh was able to convey the spirit of the

107 Hugh often referred to Father Wolohan as his "first teacher" in ministry. Despite considerable differences in age and ideology, the two became lifelong friends. As a seminarian assigned to Sacred Heart Parish, where Hugh was in residence and later co-pastor, I recall Hugh's frequent visits to Father Wolohan, who, in retirement, lived in a small home in the Sixteen Acres section of Springfield. It was a great pleasure to accompany Hugh on several of these visits.

108 Perhaps no two terms are used more frequently in studies of Vatican II than *ressourcement* and *aggiornamento.* In the context of Vatican II, *ressourcement* entails a consideration of insights gained from original sources such as the scriptures, early Church teaching, and patterns of Christian life and worship while *aggiornamento* entails a process of revitalization and renewal intended to bring institutions up to date.

109 Yves Congar (1904–1995) was a French Dominican priest and theologian. In 1937, Congar founded the *Unam Sanctum* series, which called for a "return to the sources" in an effort to set theological foundations for ecumenical dialogue. Henri Marie-Joseph de Lubac (1896–1991) was a French Jesuit priest and theologian. During WWII, de Lubac was influential in publishing *Témoignage Chrétien,* a Nazi-resistance journal. During Vatican II, de Lubac emphasized the Church as the entire People of God rather than just the hierarchy or clergy.

Council and the thought of its major contributors in a way that was accessible to the person in the pew. Saint Michael's parishioners, now well into their eighties and nineties, fondly recall attending Hugh's adult-education series as young adults and the great patience and pastoral sensitivity he demonstrated when discussing the progress of the Council or presenting the rich content of the documents it was debating. Religious sisters, parish priests, and laity who attended programs Hugh offered throughout the Diocese of Springfield during the conciliar and post-conciliar years also have fond memories of his efforts to share the spirit and work of Vatican II.[110]

During his tenure in East Longmeadow, Hugh devoted considerable thought and reflection to the documents emerging from Vatican II and their invitation to rethink the nature of priesthood and ministry.[111] It was also during those early years of ministry that Hugh began to develop important lifelong relationships with other diocesan priests. Although no single essay or retreat talk devoted exclusively to the topic of priesthood as a sacrament of friendship can be found among Hugh's many writings, allusions to this rich concept abound in his writings. More than a concept, priesthood as a sacrament of friendship is a reality Hugh embodied, especially in his ministry with and for priests.

We begin this chapter with an overview of insights on the nature of the priesthood Hugh gained from the scriptures and Church documents written during and after Vatican II. Next, we direct our attention to the ways in which the New Testament and select primary sources influenced Hugh's understanding of friendship. Finally, we consider ways in which Hugh's own priesthood of fifty-three years invited others to claim their Belovedness.[112]

---

110 The *Springfield Union* of September 10, 1969, reported that when Hugh left East Longmeadow for Louvain, where he undertook doctoral studies, more than 1,100 parishioners and friends gathered in Saint Michael's Parish Hall to express their thanks and to offer best wishes.

111 Vatican II promulgated sixteen documents. The major themes of these documents were further developed in a series of post-conciliar documents. For complete texts of the original sixteen documents translated in inclusive language, see *Vatican II: Constitutions, Decrees, Declarations,* ed. Austin Flannery, OP (Northport, NY: Costello Publishing Company, 1996).

112 Henri Nouwen, a Dutch Catholic priest and theologian, spoke frequently of what it means for people to claim their true identity as "God's Beloved."

PRIESTHOOD

INSIGHTS FROM NEW TESTAMENT

In a paper prepared shortly after returning to the Diocese of Springfield from the University of Louvain, where he received dual doctorates in theology (STD and PhD), Hugh reflects on the three priesthoods evidenced in the New Testament.[113] This relatively short paper, which Hugh frequently adapted and delivered as a retreat talk, speaks first of the priority given to the priesthood of Jesus Christ. Next, the paper discusses the priesthood of all believers called to follow and imitate Christ. Finally, the paper directs its attention to the ordained priesthood. This third priesthood Hugh refers to as "a priesthood of altar and sacrifice."[114]

In his reflections on these three priesthoods, Hugh was especially influenced by the work of Father Raymond Brown, a member of the Society of the Priests of Saint Sulpice and biblical scholar on the faculty of Saint Mary's Seminary during Hugh's student days.[115] Careful study of Brown's exegesis of the Letter to the Hebrews and participation in seminary courses taught by Brown led Hugh to acknowledge the primacy Hebrews affords to the priesthood of Jesus Christ. In this regard, Hugh directs his readers' attention to Hebrews 4:14–16: "Therefore, since we have a great high priest who has ascended into heaven, Jesus the Son of God, let us hold firmly to the faith we profess." Following the lead of Brown and other scripture scholars, Hugh refers to the priesthood of Jesus Christ as the "first priesthood."[116]

In commenting on the Letter to the Hebrews, Hugh is quick to point out that although Hebrews insists on the uniqueness of Christ's priesthood, it also emphasizes that priesthood was something conferred on Jesus, not something he sought out in an act of self-aggrandizement. Here, Hugh cites Hebrews 5:5: "In the same way, Christ did not take on himself the glory of becoming a high priest."

---

113 Hugh F. Crean, "The Three Biblical Priesthoods," 1977.

114 Crean, 3.

115 In his retirement years, Hugh prepared a list of teachers who influenced him most. Two biblical scholars, Father Raymond Brown, SS, and Father Lawrence Dannemiller, SS, are the seminary faculty members credited by Hugh with having a lasting impact on his priesthood and scholarship.

116 Crean, 2.

Hugh concludes his study of this first priesthood by pointing to Hebrews 5:8 and its reminder that Jesus "learned obedience from what he suffered." Hugh asserts that it is in terms of obedience and compassionate suffering that the ordained priest is invited to imitate Christ the High Priest.[117]

While recognizing the primacy accorded to the priesthood of Jesus Christ, of particular interest to Hugh is the priesthood of all believers. Biblical support for this second priesthood is found in 1 Peter 2:9, which reminds a largely Christian audience that they are "a chosen race, a royal priesthood, a holy nation, God's own people." Greatly influenced by Brown's exegesis of this passage, Hugh encourages us to understand this second priesthood in terms of a covenantal relationship characterized by a call to holiness rather than in terms of cultic practice or priestly function associated today with ordained ministry.

Adding credence to the importance of this second, or universal, priesthood of all believers is the fact that nowhere in the New Testament is any individual Christian designated as a *presbyteros,* or priest, in the sense of one who is ordained, offers sacrifice, or governs. Hugh points out that on the relatively few occasions when the term *presbyteros* is used in the New Testament, it refers simply to an elder among the people.

Brown, Hugh's mentor, offers valuable insight on the hesitancy of New Testament writers to refer to any one member of this new Christian community as a priest. As Brown explains, early Christians saw themselves as the renewed Israel, differing only in some features, including the belief that Jesus was the Messiah. They did not yet see themselves as the new Israel. In Brown's estimation, "these early Christians acknowledged the Jewish priesthood as valid and therefore never thought of a priesthood of their own."[118]

Following Brown's lead, Hugh suggests that before a special Christian priesthood could emerge, two things had to occur. First, Christians had to come to think of themselves as a new religion distinct from Judaism. Second, Christianity had to have a sacrifice at which this new priesthood could preside.[119] If we follow this logic, three factors contributed to the emergence of Christianity as a religion

117 Crean, 5.

118 Raymond Brown, *Priest and Bishop: Biblical Reflections* (Eugene, OR: Wipf & Stock Publishers, 1970), 17.

119 See Brown, 17–19.

unto itself: (1) the destruction of the Temple in the year 50 CE, (2) the increasing dominance of non-Jews joining the Jesus movement, and (3) divisive, self-destructive factions within Judaism. Only with the death of Jesus and a growing understanding of the Eucharist as an unbloody sacrifice did the need emerge for a priesthood entrusted with offering the new sacrifice we call the Eucharist.

In commenting on this third priesthood of altar and sacrifice, Hugh notes that even though the apostles and their successors presided over the Eucharistic sacrifice, the title "priest" was not used until later in Church history:

> Recent studies of Christian worship insist that it was not until the end of the second century that the term "priest" began to be applied in a special way to the Christian minister of the Eucharist. Even then, the Eucharistic priesthood does not supplant the priesthood of all believers in Christian parlance. Only in the third and fourth centuries can one begin to take for granted that when "priests" are mentioned the author is thinking specifically of the ordained minister of the Eucharist.[120]

Hugh is convinced that lessons learned from a study of the historical development of this third priesthood necessarily modify our traditional understanding of the blanket claim that Jesus instituted the priesthood at the Last Supper. Although some historical roots and nuances for the institution of an ordained priesthood are found in the Last Supper account, the priesthood of all believers retained its central importance in New Testament times.

According to Hugh, this emphasis on the common priesthood of all believers is supported by the fact that in the Gospel of John, written more than a decade after the other three gospels, there is no narrative memorializing the institution of the Eucharist at the Last Supper. More poignantly, there is no mention of Jesus blessing and sharing bread and wine. Instead, we find Jesus washing the feet of his disciples and telling them that as he has done for them, so they must do for one another. Following Brown's lead, Hugh believes that John's focus on the washing

120 Crean, 4.

of the feet, rather than on the blessing and sharing of bread and wine, was both intentional and corrective:

> If, by the time the fourth evangelist wrote, there was already a deep vernation for Eucharist, there may have already been a sense of privilege associated with it. Although many might vie to preside at the Eucharist, few would really want to wash one another's feet.[121]

As Hugh points out, without the sense of service associated with John's narrative of the Last Supper, we would be left with a distorted understanding of what the New Testament wants to tell us about priesthood. Hugh finds support for this connection between priesthood and service in important conciliar and post-conciliar documents.

INSIGHTS FROM KEY CONCILIAR DOCUMENTS

In the Winter 2012 edition of *Seminary Journal,* Jesuit priest Thomas Rausch suggests that although Vatican II did much to renew our understanding of the role of bishops and laity in the Church, the Council was woefully deficient in its treatises on priesthood and religious life.[122] To support this contention, Rausch appeals to theologian Peter Hünermann, who called *Presbyterorum ordinis,* the Council's Decree on Priestly Life and Ministry, "one of the Council's stepchildren."[123]

In defense of *Presbyterorum ordinis,* Rausch reminds us that the document was never intended to present a theology of the priesthood or ministry, per se.[124] Rather, the document was originally intended to deal with Church discipline as it relates to such things as the relationship between priests and bishops. Despite considerable criticism of the document, Rausch suggests that

121 Crean, 5.

122 Thomas Raush, SJ, "Vatican II on the Priesthood: Fifty Years Later." *Seminary Journal* 12, Winter 2012.

123 Peter Hunermann, "The Weeks of the Council," *History of Vatican II, Vol V,* ed. Giuseppe Alberigo and Joseph Komanchak (Maryknoll, NY: Orbis, 2006), 457.

124 Documents of Vatican II. *Presbyterorum ordinis* (Decree on the Life and Ministry of Priests), December 1965. https://www.vatican.va/archive/hist_councils/ii_vatican_council/documents/vat-ii_decree_19651207_presbyterorum-ordinis_en.html

the final draft of the document includes an abundance of positive approaches to priesthood and ministry. These positive approaches become apparent when *Presbyterorum ordinis,* promulgated in 1965, is read in the context of *Lumen gentium,* the Dogmatic Constitution on the Church, which had been promulgated in 1964.[125]

At this juncture, it is important to note that in retreat conferences for priests, seminary presentations, and public lectures, Hugh frequently cited Rausch. It is also important to note that, in his work with priests, *Lumen gentium* and *Presbyterorum ordinis* are the conciliar documents to which Hugh refers most frequently. These two documents, along with *Gaudium et spes,* the Pastoral Constitution on the Church in the Modern World, spoke to the depths of Hugh's mind and soul.[126] In many of the late-night conversations Hugh and I enjoyed while living together in Sacred Heart Rectory, he referred to these conciliar documents and the ways they shaped his understanding of the priesthood. Although *Gaudium et spes* affords rich insight into the "joys and hopes, griefs and anxieties" within which all ministry is exercised in today's Church, it is in *Lumen gentium* and *Presbyterorum ordinis* that we find the most explicit conciliar teachings on the essence and form of the priesthood in today's Church.

LUMEN GENTIUM

Lumen gentium, like all conciliar documents, was an evolving document. Bishops and their theological advisors carefully reviewed and revised various drafts of the document prepared by a subcommittee of bishops and their theological advisors before it was debated on the Council floor and eventually promulgated by Paul VI in December 1964.

In a talk delivered during the Symposium on the Future of Ministry in New England held at Mont Marie Conference Center in Holyoke, Massachusetts, in

---

125 Documents of Vatican II. *Lumen Gentium* (The Dogmatic Constitution on the Church), December 1964. https://www.vatican.va/archive/hist_councils/ii_vatican_council/documents/vat-ii_const_19641121_lumen-gentium_en.html

126 Documents of Vatican II. *Gaudium et spes* (The Pastoral Constitution on the Church in the Modern World), December 1965. https://www.vatican.va/archive/hist_councils/ii_vatican_council/documents/vat-ii_const_19651207_gaudium-et-spes_en.html

October 1984, Hugh discusses the various drafts, or schemas, of *Lumen gentium*.[127] He points out that the earliest drafts of *Lumen gentium* began with an exploration of the hierarchical structure of the Church rather than with a consideration of the centrality of Baptism held in common by the entire People of God.

Hugh stresses that, following interventions by Yves Congar and other theological advisors, the proposed chapter order was eventually changed. As a result of these insightful interventions, the final draft of *Lumen gentium* addresses the hierarchical structure of the Church only after it has first considered the mystery of the Church and its Trinitarian roots in Chapter I and the primacy afforded to the entire People of God in Chapter II.

In Chapter II, *Lumen gentium* recovers the theology of the charisms (e.g., teaching, prophesying, governing, etc.) mentioned in many of Saint Paul's writings and evidenced in the life of the earliest Christian communities. This chapter also teaches that laypersons are sacramentally "commissioned" to share in the Church's saving ministry through Baptism and Confirmation.[128] Perhaps most importantly, Chapter II affirms that the common priesthood of the faithful and the ministerial priesthood of the ordained share in the one priesthood of Christ, who is at once priest, prophet, and king.[129]

Lumen gentium not only mentions this threefold office of Jesus and the ways the faithful and ordained share in these three roles or functions of teaching, governing, and sanctifying. *Lumen gentium* made these three functions of teaching, governing, and sanctifying the very structure for its theology of ministry.[130] This structure of ministry would find further development in *Presbyterorum ordinis.*

PRESBYTERORUM ORDINIS

Rausch undertakes his study of *Presbyterorum ordinis* with the assertion that, from a doctrinal perspective, this document did not intend to go beyond *Lumen gentium*. Rausch concurs with John O'Malley, a Jesuit priest and noted

127 Hugh F. Crean, "Roots and Realities of a Priestly People." *The Future of Ministry: The New England Symposium Papers* (New York: William H. Sadlier, 1985).

128 *Lumen Gentium*, ¶33.

129 *Lumen gentium*, ¶10.

130 Kenan Osborne, *Priesthood: A History of the Ordained Ministry in the Roman Catholic Church* (Eugene, OR: Wipf & Stock Publishers, 1989), 312.

Church historian, who asserts that *Presbyterorum ordinis* chose to treat priesthood primarily in the framework of ministry and service, rather than sacramental power.[131] In this regard, the document begins by stating that in Jesus, "all faithful are made a royal and holy priesthood."[132] As Rausch emphasizes, the context for the ministry of the ordained is the priesthood of the faithful that it serves.

The word "ministry" appears forty-five times in *Presbyterorum ordinis.* The documents place particular emphasis on the priest's ministry of preaching the Word. The document also stresses the importance of the priest being formed by the Word of God he preaches. *Presbyterorum ordinis* reminds readers that while exercising the role of father and teacher among the People of God, priests are also brothers to all reborn at the font of Baptism.[133]

Hugh expands on Rausch's commentary on *Presbyterorum ordinis* to assert that as father, teacher, and brother to all reborn in Baptism, the priest is perhaps the most crucial enabler of the ministry of others:

> On the local scene, the priest can open many doors for the other ministers or close them tightly to the detriment of the other ministers and the local Church. He [the priest] needs a selflessness and a sense of security to know that his role as a priest is not threatened or compromised with the collaborative inclusion of others; rather, his role is clarified and enhanced as all work together to build the Kingdom.[134]

As we conclude this brief exploration of ways in which *Lumen gentium* and *Presbyterorum ordinis* understand the nature of the ordained priesthood, we must emphasize that, in both "The Three Biblical Priesthoods" and "Roots and Realities of a Priestly People," Hugh stresses that neither *Lumen gentium* nor *Presbyterorum ordinis* intended to degrade the special dignity of the ministerial, or ordained, priesthood. In fact, *Presbyterorum ordinis* appeals

---

131 John O'Malley, *What Happened at Vatican II* (Cambridge, MA: Harvard University Press, 2008), 273.

132 *Presbyterorum ordinis*, ¶2.

133 *Presbyterorum ordinis*, ¶9.

134 Crean, "Roots and Realities of a Priestly People," 23.

to the language of Scholasticism and insists that, in preaching the Word and celebrating the sacraments, the priest acts *in persona Christi* (in the person of Christ).[135] In recognizing this priesthood of altar and sacrifice, Hugh cautioned against clericalism and any sense of entitlement sometimes presumed by the ordained.

In this regard, Cardinal Walter Kasper emphasizes that speaking and acting in the name of Jesus is a considerable challenge. In Kasper's estimation:

> One can only speak and act in the name of Jesus if one also speaks and acts in the way of Jesus . . . The offices [ordained ministries] are not the exercise of sovereignty and power, but by following Jesus, they are service for the people of God and its mission . . . They [priests] are not to be lords over faith but servants of joy. With the washing of the feet on the evening before his suffering and death, Jesus gave a vivid example of this servant's service.[136]

Kasper's insistence that priests exercise their sacred powers in service for the building of God's kingdom and advancement of the Church's mission resonates well with Hugh's frequent appeal in retreat conferences and academic presentations to the washing of the feet in John's gospel mentioned earlier in this chapter and to the "priestly prayer" of Jesus, found in John 14:12. In that prayer, Jesus prays that those who come after him will do even greater things than he, himself, has done.

We conclude this first section with the realization that much of Hugh's thought on the nature of the priesthood is shaped by John's gospel and its constant emphasis on radical equality as the hallmark of life among the first believers. This radical equality is evidenced in John 15:15 when Jesus says, "I no longer call you servants, for a servant does not know what his master is about. Instead, I call you my friends."

---

135 *Presbyterorum ordinis*, ¶2.

136 Walter Kasper. *The Catholic Church: Nature, Reality and Mission*, translator Thomas Hoebel (New York: Bloomsbury T&T Clark, 2015), 242.

FRIENDSHIP

INSIGHTS FROM THE NEW TESTAMENT

When reading Hugh's homilies, retreat conference notes, and more formal talks, the reader is immediately struck by the many times Hugh speaks about friendship, particularly in the context of priestly fraternity.

Hugh's friendship of more than thirty-five years with his childhood friend Jim Andrews informed the many rich friendships Hugh enjoyed with people from all walks of life. As Sister Jane Morrissey intimates in her contribution to this book, it was from each other that Hugh and Jim learned how to be a friend to others.

As he grew older, Hugh's appreciation of the friendships he enjoyed with others was greatly informed by Henri Nouwen, a Dutch-born Catholic priest, theologian, teacher, and writer. Hugh often quoted Nouwen and encouraged friends to read Nouwen.

I vividly recall an extended conversation Hugh and I enjoyed in the summer of 1994 while I was home on break from doctoral studies in Washington, DC. The conversation was about Nouwen's recently published book *Life of the Beloved.*[137] The book touched Hugh's spirit. By extension, it touched mine.

In *Life of the Beloved,* Nouwen asks the all-important question that remains with me today: "Isn't that what friendship is all about: giving each other the gift of our Belovedness?"[138]

Hugh spoke often about the connection between friendship and Belovedness. In doing so, he relied heavily on learnings gained from the New Testament. As we shall see, Hugh was most profoundly influenced by the poetic language and rich imagery of John's gospel.

In an informative essay on friendship in the New Testament, Australian theologian Sean Winter suggests that the language of friendship found in

137 Henri Nouwen, *Life of the Beloved: Spiritual Living in a Secular World* (New York: Crossroad Books, 1992).

138 Nouwen, 3

the New Testament traces its roots to early Greek literature and the ways that literature describes forms of intimate association between two or more people.[139]

In the New Testament friendship tradition, *phil*, the Greek root of "friend," was used to indicate possession (belonging to me) or affection (being loved by me). Although underdeveloped in the New Testament, the early Greek tradition also used *phil* when speaking of friendship as a gift or reflection of the divine.

We begin this brief overview of friendship in the New Testament with the letters written by Saint Paul that place considerable emphasis on the horizontal dimension of friendship.

THE PAULINE LETTERS

There is no debating the fact that when considering the New Testament as a whole, Paul's letters contain the most frequent and sustained reflections on friendship. To be even more specific, it is in Paul's letter to the Philippians that we find the most extensive reference to friendship and friendship-related themes. Paul's use of "partnership" as a simile for "friendship" in Philippians 1:5, 2:1; 4:14–15 is important in this regard. Also important is Paul's mention of what it means for believers, called as friends, to act in "one spirit":

> Only, conduct yourselves in a way worthy of the gospel of Christ, so that, whether I come and see you or am absent, I may hear news of you, that you are standing firm in one spirit, with one mind struggling together for the faith of the gospel.[140]

Paul's admonition for believers to conduct themselves in a way worthy of the gospel must be read in the context of Philippians 2. In Philippians 2:2, Paul encourages believers not only to conduct themselves in a certain way but to complete his joy "by being of the same mind, with the same love, united in heart, thinking one thing."

---

139 Sean Winter, "Friendship Traditions in the New Testament: An Overview," *Pacifica* 29 (2016), 3.

140 Phil. 1:27.

GOSPEL OF JOHN

The Gospel of John regularly uses two verbs when speaking of love: *phileō* and *agapaō.* Whereas *phileō* usually refers to affection or friendship among equals intimated in early Greek friendship literature, *agapaō* refers to God's love for his children, the love between husband and wife, and the love between parent and child.

John 15:12–15 gives us the clearest clue as to how John appropriated the friendship traditions common in the New Testament. In John's gospel, Jesus is the model of friendship. He is the one who "will lay down his life for his friends" (John 15:13). Jesus is also the one who invites the disciples to imitate his love: "Love one another as I have loved you" (John 15:12).

Underlying the rich theology of friendship found in John's gospel is the conviction that the love that binds Jesus with his disciples is the same love by which the disciples are brought into a relationship not only with each other but also with God.

Gail O'Day, professor of theology at Chandler School of Theology, reminds us that the type of friendship to which Jesus invites his disciples does not happen overnight. According to O'Day, "the title 'friend' becomes something into which Jesus invites his disciples to grow."[141] The disciples are challenged to embody day in and day out the life-giving sacrifice Jesus modeled for them. Jesus' ultimate gift of his life for others defines the ultimate meaning and the extent of the love to which true friends are invited.

The evolving stages of friendship to which O'Day alludes are emphasized in a treatise on friendship by Aelred of Rievaulx, a twelfth-century monk.

AELRED OF RIEVAULX

Aelred of Rievaulx (1110–1167) was a monk and abbot who lived in the Golden Age of Cistercian reform. He founded the new abbey of Rievaulx in England and soon attracted more than six hundred monks to join him.

Aelred was a gifted orator and writer. His masterpiece, *Spiritual Friendship,* explores ways in which true friendships model the intimacy to which Jesus invites his disciples in John's gospel. Seminarians of Hugh's era were regularly

141 Gail R. O'Day, "Jesus as Friend in the Gospel of John," *Interpretation* 58, no. 2 (2004), 152.

introduced to the work of Aelred in spiritual conferences and as part of their study of ascetical theology.

As spiritual writer Susan Muto points out in an essay that appeared in *Human Development,* Aelred goes to great length to distinguish fair-weather acquaintances from real friends.[142] Aelred is convinced that in the company of real friends, we overcome self-centeredness and rejoice in another's accomplishment without a trace of envy.

Like the evangelist John, Aelred believes that true friendships are characterized by horizontal and vertical dimensions. In true friendships, we grow closer to others and closer to God. True friendships begin in time but are perfected in eternity.

When we apply Aelred's thought on spiritual friendship to priestly life and ministry in today's Church, we can say that the capacity for mature spiritual friendships is an essential measure of healthy human formation for priests. As John Celichowski, OFM Cap, Director of Formation for the Capuchin Province of Saint Joseph, emphasizes, mature friendships sustain vocations and are key to a priest's happiness.[143] Whereas formators once encouraged candidates for ministry to be more detached from "particular friendships" with one or two others in order to give themselves more fully to God and the service of the Church, the *Program for Priestly Formation* now insists that an ability to build and maintain healthy friendships is an essential element of personal integration and ministry to and with the People of God.[144]

First published in 1992 by the United States Conference of Catholic Bishops, the *Program for Priestly Formation* to which Celichowski alludes, along with John Paul II's apostolic exhortation, *Pastores dabo vobis* (I Will Give You Shepherds), also published in 1992, informed much of the work Hugh did in conjunction with the International Institute for Clergy Formation.[145] Housed on the campus of Seton Hall University in New Jersey, the Institute was founded in 1987 by Hugh's close

142 Susan Muto, "Aelred of Rievaulx on Spiritual Friendship," *Human Development* 39, no. 3 (Spring 2019), 40–47.

143 John Celichowski, "Friendship and Human Formation," *Human Development* 39, no. 3 (Spring 2019), 33.

144 United States Conference of Catholic Bishops, *Program of Priestly Formation,* 5th ed. June 2005. https://www.usccb.org/upload/program-priestly-formation-fifth-edition.pdf

145 John-Paul II, *Pastores dabo vobis* (I Will Give You Shepherds). March 1992. https://www.vatican.va/content/john-paul-ii/it/apost_exhortations/documents/hf_jp-ii_exh_25031992_pastores-dabo-vobis.html

friend and colleague Monsignor Andrew (Andy) Cusack. Since its foundation, more than ten thousand priests from around the world have participated in programs offered under the auspices of the institute.[146]

It was my great pleasure to first meet Andy, a priest of the nearby Diocese of Bridgeport, Connecticut, during one of his many visits to Sacred Heart Rectory. It was an even greater pleasure to be part of many rich conversations Hugh, Andy, and I shared along with George Farland, who, as Sister Mary Johnson tells us, was in team ministry with Hugh at Sacred Heart Parish. I vividly recall the excitement Andy and Hugh demonstrated when the two documents just mentioned were published.

Although any detailed analysis of these two documents is beyond the scope of this chapter, we briefly note that both documents emphasize the Trinitarian foundations of ordained ministry and the communitarian form of life to which the ordained are invited. According to *The Program for Priestly Formation,* this invitation means that priests "ought to develop and foster bonds of fraternity and cooperation among themselves, so that the reality of the presbyterate may take hold of their lives."[147]

As we shall see in the next and final section of this chapter, Hugh was described by those who knew him best as a "priest's priest." Through decades of tireless work with and for priests, the reality of priesthood "took hold" of Hugh's life. In this process, Hugh's priesthood became a sacrament of friendship not only with his brother priests but also with countless religious and laity.

PRIESTHOOD, SACRAMENT, BELOVEDNESS

Earlier in this chapter, we noted that Vatican II was characterized by a twofold effort to restore and reform. In this process, no theological concept received greater scrutiny and reflection than the concept of sacrament.

146 A link to audio recordings of talks delivered in conjunction with the Summer Institute, including talks given by Hugh, is found in the appendix.

147 United States Conference of Catholic Bishops, *Program of Priestly Formation,* ¶18.

Vatican II's very first constitution was promulgated in 1963. The document is known as *Sacrosanctum concilium* (The Constitution on the Sacred Liturgy).[148] This important constitution goes to great length to retrieve an appreciation of the seven sacraments as sacred signs revelatory of God's love. However, it is in the Council's second constitution, *Lumen gentium* (The Dogmatic Constitution on the Church), that we witness the Council's most concerted effort to appropriate and then expand on the patristic notion of sacrament.

Lumen gentium and the rich pastoral and theological reflection that has taken place in its aftermath encourage us to understand the word "sacrament" in terms of something even more foundational than the seven sacraments. Scholars of the Council, including Karl Rahner, insist that a sacrament is a sacred sign revelatory of God's presence.[149] Collectively, these scholars suggest that human existence and the friendships we enjoy must be seen as a sacrament, or sacred sign, of God's presence in our life.

Central to an integral understanding of the term "sacrament" in Catholic thought is the conviction that all sacraments operate on two levels. As sacred signs, sacraments not only point to the mystery of God's love; they also make that love present. To refer to priesthood as a sacrament of friendship is to assert that priesthood is a sacred sign that simultaneously points to and makes present the Belovedness inferred by Jesus when he calls us his friends.[150]

In the years that have transpired since Hugh's death in 2015, Sister Joan Ryzewicz, now president of the Sisters of St. Joseph of Springfield and one of Hugh's closest friends and confidants, has often reflected on the important role friendships played in Hugh's life. Hugh recognized that human love and friendship draw us deeper and deeper into the mystery of God. As Sister Joan points out, Hugh also knew that human love and friendship also draw

---

148 Vatican II Documents. *Sacrosanctum Concilium* (The Constitution on the Sacred Liturgy). December 1963. https://www.vatican.va/archive/hist_councils/ii_vatican_council/documents/vat-ii_const_19631204_sacrosanctum-concilium_en.html

149 Karl Rahner (1904–1984) was a Jesuit priest and theologian. For a very helpful overview of Karl Rahner's thought, see Leo O'Donovan (ed). *A World of Grace: An Introduction to the Themes and Foundations of Karl Rahner's Theology* (Washington, DC: Georgetown University Press, 1995).

150 John 15:14.

us deeper and deeper into the mystery of what it is to be human and what it means to be friends.

To no small degree, Hugh's reflections on priesthood as a sacred sign of friendship were shaped by his reading of Bernard Cooke, whose distinguished career as sacramental theologian included a professorship at Hugh's alma mater, the College of the Holy Cross.[151] Particularly appealing to Hugh was Cooke's insistence that human friendship is, itself, "a basic sacrament."[152]

FRIENDSHIP: A BASIC SACRAMENT

Human love and friendship draw us deeper and deeper into the mystery of God. At the same time, human love and friendship draw us deeper and deeper into the mystery of what it is to be human and what it means to be friends. According to Cooke, "being truly personal with and for one another is sacramental; it is a revelation of our humanity at the same time that it is a revelation of God."[153]

In the many homilies delivered on the occasion of a priest's first Mass, a religious sister's profession of vows, or celebrations of special anniversaries of ordination or religious profession, Hugh spoke of the unique friendship he enjoyed with the person being honored that day. Hugh also referenced these and other life-giving friendships in funeral homilies he delivered for friends from all walks of life.

Hugh realized that friendships are transformative. Friendships allow us to care for others. Friendships allow others to care for us. Friends invite each other to be their best selves.

Like his mentor, Paul Tillich, Hugh had a unique way of letting his friends know that they were accepted.[154]

---

151 I still have in my library several of Cooke's books that Hugh generously gave me when he moved to his retirement residence at Providence Place in Holyoke, Massachusetts.

152 Bernard Cooke, "Human Friendship: Basic Sacrament," *Boston College: Church in the 21st Century Resources.* Fall 2007.

153 Cooke, 3–4.

154 Paul Tillich, "You Are Accepted," in *The Shaking of the Foundations* (Eugene, OR: Wipf & Stock Publishers, 1948), 153–63.

SACRED HEART RECTORY: A SCHOOL OF FRIENDSHIP

Monsignor George Farland, who continues to serve as pastor of Sacred Heart Parish in Springfield, Massachusetts, and I learned much about friendship from Hugh. Hugh and I were twenty-one years apart in age and ordination; George and I are fifteen years apart in age and ordination. Although Hugh and George were closer on many levels because of proximity in age and the sheer length of time they lived and ministered together, both invited me into their friendship. Along with the Sisters of Notre Dame assigned to the parish and wonderful parishioners mentioned by Sister Mary Johnson earlier in this book, Hugh and George became my first teachers in ministry. To use a rather playful expression Hugh frequently relied on when referring to those personal qualities and practices that make for effective priestly ministry, Hugh and George modeled "priest-craft" for me. They showed me what it was to be a parish priest in a Church awakened to new life by Vatican II. They taught me the things no seminary can teach. They introduced me to what *Presbyterorum ordinis* calls "the intimate sacramental fraternity" of priesthood.[155]

In a formal instruction issued in 2016 by the Congregation for the Clergy on the formation of priests, it is noted that the sacramental fraternity *Presbyterorum ordinis* first envisioned for priests is fostered by many things, including spiritual direction, the communal celebration of the Eucharist, and formal gatherings of priests.[156] The Congregation for the Clergy goes even further. It insists that sacramental fraternity is also fostered in less formal ways. These less formal ways include the sharing of a common table and a common life.

It was through the sharing of a common life and around a common table that my friendship with Hugh and George grew. At Sacred Heart Rectory, I learned that all healthy friendships invite us to conversion and change.

It was in the context of a common life and shared table that Hugh and George first intervened and then accompanied me on my own journey from addiction to recovery. I am just one of many who knew firsthand their unique ability to "be

155 *Presbyterorum ordinis*, ¶14.

156 Congregation for the Clergy, *Ratio fundamentalis institutionis sacerdotalis* (The Gift of the Priestly Vocation), 2016, ¶88. http://www.clerus.va/content/dam/clerus/Ratio%20Fundamentalis/The%20Gift%20of%20the%20Priestly%20Vocation.pdf

there" for friends, especially when, in the words of Buddhist monk Pema Chōdrōn, "things fall apart."[157]

WHEN THINGS FALL APART

At several junctures in this book, it has been noted that Hugh served for many years in diocesan positions that entailed ministry to priests. Sister Mary Johnson tells us that these positions included Vicar for Clergy and Director of Priest Personnel. In these and other significant appointments, Hugh's priesthood became a sacred sign of friendship to priests facing personal and ministerial struggles.

Hugh embodied the good things that close friends do for one another. He knew how to say hard things in a caring and empathetic way.

Paul Wadell, professor of theology and religious studies at Saint Norbert's University in Wisconsin, reminds us of some of the many good things that friends do for one another:

> Friends bring joy and hope and meaning to our lives. When life throws us more than we can possibly bear, our friends are there to comfort, encourage, and support us. When we fail, fall short, and do things of which we are ashamed, rather than giving up on us, friends insist on loving us until we fulfill our capabilities.[158]

Very early in my priesthood, it became apparent to Hugh, George, and others that my life and ministry were being negatively impacted because of my drinking. As a true friend, Hugh saw things that untreated alcoholism made it impossible for me to see. As Vicar for Clergy, Hugh knew his responsibility to say the hard things friends sometimes have to say. He recognized the urgency of getting me the type of help I desperately needed.

That help first came in the form of extended heart-to-heart conversations that began sometime in the winter of 1991. During those conversations, Hugh innately sensed that I did not find the routine of day-to-day parish ministry

---

157 Pema Chōdrōn, *When Things Fall Apart: Heart Advice for Difficult Times* (Boulder, CO: Shambhala Publications, 2000).

158 Paul Wadell, "Fashioned for Friendship," *Human Development*, 39, no. 3 (2019), 7.

to be sufficiently fulfilling. Although I had already begun teaching one or two courses a semester at Elms College, Hugh felt I needed to be more deeply engaged in teaching and studying theology. As a result, Hugh suggested to college and diocesan officials that I be released in the fall of 1992 for doctoral studies in theology. In the meantime, Hugh asked me to begin meeting regularly with Father John Johnson, a man whose tall and imposing physique were outdone only by his gentle and kind spirit.[159]

John ("Johnny") Johnson was Hugh's close friend and confidant. John held a doctorate in theology from the North American College in Rome and was the founding director of the diocesan marriage counseling office. He was deeply admired by his brother priests and regularly hosted Friday night clergy gatherings in his West Springfield rectory.

John died in 2001. For forty-five years of priesthood, John counseled people from every walk of life. As a counselor, John accompanied many people struggling with addiction. Although not in recovery himself, John believed in the principles of Twelve Step recovery. He was convinced that treatment works and that recovery is possible.

In the homily he delivered at John's funeral, Hugh recalls John's habit of embracing friends "with a bear hug of Cursillo bravado."[160] It was with "bear hug bravado" that John welcomed me into his life. John planted in my mind the thought that the apparent problem in my life (excessive drinking) might not be the only problem. He strongly suggested that I consider working with a therapist and attending meetings of Alcoholics Anonymous.

The journey of healing to which recovery invites us is long and often circuitous. When it became obvious that I needed time away from doctoral studies and teaching to get sober and focus solely on recovery, I recall Hugh's reassuring words. He invited me to see the summer I would spend at Guest House, a Michigan-based residential treatment center for clergy and religious, as "a short detour" on the road of life and ministry. Most of all, Hugh assured me that our God often comes to us in the darkness, including the darkness of addiction.

---

159 Father Johnson served as one of the parish priests assigned to Hugh's home parish during Hugh's childhood. John served as one of the assisting priests at Hugh's First Mass.

160 Hugh F. Crean. Funeral Homily. Monsignor John Johnson. July 5, 2001.

When I returned home from Guest House in time to begin the fall semester at the Elms, Hugh repeatedly urged me to be gentle with myself. He reminded me that early recovery and reentry to ministry are never easy. Hugh made me promise to make recovery my priority.

Chōdrōn tells us that things falling apart and coming together again is a kind of testing and a kind of healing. Hugh's friendship helped me find the healing I so desperately sought. Hugh's friendship invited me to claim my Belovedness.

CLAIMING OUR BELOVEDNESS

Hugh's priesthood invited countless others like me to claim their Belovedness. Whether in the pulpit, the confessional, or classroom, he helped others claim their identity as God's Beloved. Wherever he ministered, Hugh helped people see that the blessings we give each other in life are "expressions of the blessing that rests on us from all eternity."[161]

Hugh had a unique ability to celebrate the expressions of God's blessings he recognized in others. He loved to laugh at a good joke. He loved to watch the antics of Thomasine O'Connor as she danced and sang her way into the hearts of the parishioners to whom she ministered at Sacred Heart. Hugh loved to laugh at himself. Nothing made him happier than sharing a meal and playing cards with priest-friends on Wednesday afternoons. Humorous stories emerging from an annual January getaway to Puerto Rico with the likes of Fathers George Farland, Dan Doyle, Dan Foley, and Howard McCormick—all true characters and legends of the Diocese of Springfield—amused Hugh all year long.

CONCLUSION

Hugh's lighthearted and gregarious side was a side many people never really knew. They only saw the reverent celebrant of Mass, gifted homilist, college professor, retreat master, or diocesan official. On more than one occasion, Hugh told me that he regretted this fact. He wished that more people knew his lighter, more playful side.

161 Henri Nouwen, *Discernment: Reading the Signs of Daily Life* (New York: Harper Collins Publishers, 2013), 135.

Like most of us, Hugh wrestled with that deceiving inner voice that often wants to tell us we are not good enough. This became especially apparent in the months and years following a diagnosis of Alzheimer's in 2004.

Following that diagnosis, Hugh often wrote short notes to himself. Written in the very fine penmanship for which he was known, these notes were scattered among the handwritten and typed material Hugh wanted desperately to see published. In most of these notes, he expressed disappointment with himself and what he perceived as a lack of productivity on his part:

> I am now 74 years old.
> I am tired, lazy, uncertain, and only slowly productive.
> I have good material, but I must put forth more energy to move forward and produce.
> I have the tools and the material (all my own writing) to move forward and produce at least some product before I am too old.

This frustration with self was most apparent when Hugh realized he was no longer able to carry on as pastor of Our Lady of the Blessed Sacrament Parish. In a letter written in April 2004, Hugh informed Bishop Timothy McDonnell of the results of recently completed neurological testing. In that same letter, Hugh offered his resignation:

> To resign, according to Webster, is "to give up one's office" or "to withdraw formally." I do not happily choose this course of action. I am a self-starter and a proud person, but I acknowledge the wisdom of doing the right thing at the right time and for the right reason.[162]

Doing the right thing at the right time and for the right reason came naturally to Hugh. To no small degree, he possessed the practical wisdom Aristotle called "prudence." Hugh demonstrated an ability to deliberate well and then make informed choices.

162 Hugh Crean, Letter of Resignation Addressed to Bishop Timothy McDonnell, April 19, 2004.

First as a seminarian and later as a young priest, Hugh was able to measure the biblical and conciliar images of priesthood surveyed in the first section of this chapter against the true needs of God's people and the primacy of the baptismal vocation. Gifted with practical wisdom, Hugh intuitively sensed what priesthood should look and feel like in our times. As a result, he embodied a priesthood informed by Jesus' washing of his disciples' feet and his final prayer that the ones who came after would do even greater things than he.[163]

Something similar can be said of friendship. Hugh took delight in the biblical images of friendship presented in the second section of this chapter. He read learned treatises on friendship, such as that of Aelred of Rievaulx. He studied and internalized Church documents on the topic, particularly documents that addressed friendship in the context of priesthood. Hugh's gift of practical wisdom enabled him to measure all that these sources had to say against his own lived experience of friendship. In this regard, no friendship was more significant than the friendship Hugh and Jim Andrews enjoyed. In that friendship, Hugh and Jim allowed the true Belovedness of the other to shine forth.

As we saw in section three, Hugh's priesthood was a special gift to his brother priests, particularly priests like me who struggled with difficulties of any kind. His priesthood was a saving leaven for countless priests who attended one or more of the many retreats Hugh offered during twenty-five years on the retreat circuit. In the context of those retreats, Hugh had a unique way of helping priests make sense of who they were as individuals and what it meant to be a priest in the midst of a Church emerging from Vatican II.

Hugh's priesthood also impacted countless others who, in Hugh's presence, felt accepted and understood. Couples separated by divorce, single parents, and persons struggling with their sexual identity sought Hugh's guidance. A generation of Elms students delighted in Hugh's good looks and easygoing, approachable nature. Women religious whose congregations were undergoing the often painful process of renewal and reform following Vatican II still recall Hugh's compassion and willingness to accompany them. He encouraged these women to explore new vistas and new ministries. Hugh instilled in them a sense of dignity and purpose.

163 See John 14:12.

As we pointed out in this chapter, sacraments are sacred signs that make present the reality to which they point. Hugh's priesthood of more than five decades pointed to and made present the Belovedness he found in everyone he met.

And so we end this chapter and this book with a twofold promise: a promise to honor Hugh's memory by claiming our own Belovedness and a promise to help others claim their Belovedness.

After all, isn't this what priesthood, life, and friendship are really all about: helping each other claim the Belovedness that has been ours from all eternity?

REFERENCES

Brown, Raymond. *Priest and Bishop: Biblical Reflections.* Eugene, OR: Wipf & Stock Publishers, 1970.

Celichowski, John. "Friendship and Human Formation," *Human Development* 39, no. 3 (Spring 2019).

Chōdrōn, Pema. *When Things Fall Apart: Heart Advice for Difficult Times.* Boulder, CO: Shambhala Publications, 2000.

Congregation for the Clergy. *Ratio fundamentalis institutionis sacerdotalis* (The Gift of the Priestly Vocation), 2016. http://www.clerus.va/content/dam/clerus/Ratio%20Fundamentalis/The%20Gift%20of%20the%20Priestly%20Vocation.pdf

Cooke, Bernard. "Human Friendship: A Basic Sacrament," *Boston College: Church in the 21st Century Resources*, Fall 2007.

Crean, Hugh F. Funeral Homily for Monsignor John Johnson, July 5, 2001.

Crean, Hugh F. Letter of Resignation Addressed to Bishop Timothy McDonnell, April 19, 2004.

Crean, Hugh F. "Roots and Realities of a Priestly People," in *The Future of Ministry: The New England Symposium Papers*. New York: William H. Sadlier, 1985.

Crean, Hugh F. "The Three Biblical Priesthoods," 1977.

Documents of Vatican II. *Gaudium et spes* (The Pastoral Constitution on the Church in the Modern World), December 1965. https://www.vatican.va/archive/hist_councils/ii_vatican_council/documents/vat-ii_const_19651207_gaudium-et-spes_en.html

Documents of Vatican II. *Lumen gentium* (The Dogmatic Constitution on the Church), December 1964. https://www.vatican.va/archive/hist_councils/ii_vatican_council/documents/vat-ii_const_19641121_lumen-gentium_en.html

Documents of Vatican II. *Presbyterorum ordinis* (Decree on the Life and Ministry of Priests), December 1965. http://www.vatican.va/archive/hist_councils/ii_vatican_council/documents/vat-ii_decree_19651207_presbyterorum-ordinis_en.html

Documents of Vatican II. *Sacrosanctum concilium* (The Constitution on the Sacred Liturgy), December 1963. https://www.vatican.va/archive/hist_councils/ii_vatican_council/documents/vat-ii_const_19631204_sacrosanctum-concilium_en.html

Hunermann, Peter. "The Weeks of the Council," in *History of Vatican II, Vol V,* edited by Giuseppe Alberigo and Joseph Komanchak. Maryknoll, NY: Orbis, 2006.

John-Paul II. *Pastores dabo vobis* (I Will Give You Shepherds), March 1992. https://www.vatican.va/content/john-paul-ii/it/apost_exhortations/documents/hf_jp-ii_exh_25031992_pastores-dabo-vobis.html

Kasper, Walter. *The Catholic Church: Nature, Reality and Mission,* translated by Thomas Hoebel. New York: Bloomsbury T&T Clark, 2015.

Muto, Susan. "Aelred of Rievaulx on Spiritual Friendship," *Human Development* 39, no. 3 (Spring 2019).

Nouwen, Henri. *Discernment: Reading the Signs of Daily Life.* New York: Harper Collins Publishers, 2013.

Nouwen, Henri. *Life of the Beloved: Spiritual Living in a Secular World.* New York: Crossroad Books, 1992.

O'Day, Gail R. "Jesus as Friend in the Gospel of John," *Interpretation* 58, no. 2 (2004).

O'Malley, John O. *What Happened at Vatican II.* Cambridge, MA: Harvard University Press, 2008.

Osborne, Kenan. *Priesthood: A History of Ordained Ministry in the Roman Catholic Church.* Eugene, OR: Wipf & Stock Publishers, 1989.

Raush, Thomas, SJ. "Vatican II on the Priesthood: Fifty Years Later," *Seminary Journal* 12 (Winter 2012).

The *Springfield Union,* September 10, 1969.

United States Conference of Catholic Bishops. *Program of Priestly Formation, June 2005.* https://www.usccb.org/upload/program-priestly-formation-fifth-edition.pdf

Wadell, Paul. "Fashioned for Friendship," *Human Development* 39, no. 3 (Spring 2019).

Winter, Sean. "Friendship Traditions in the New Testament: An Overview," *Pacifica* 29 (2016).

Afterword

I HOPE THAT you have found this testimony and tribute to Father Hugh F. Crean as inspiring and compelling as I have. For his more than fifty years as a priest, Father Hugh's sermons, writings, and studies enlightened parishioners and scholars on their spiritual journeys.

Father Hugh was a steady presence throughout my life; I learned early on that I am his namesake. My father, James Andrews, and Father Hugh forged a lifelong friendship as high schoolers in Westfield, Massachusetts. As Father Hugh noted, my father was his "irreplaceable friend as together we snuck up on adolescence and grew to adulthood . . . Jim had all the virtues I admire and all the vices I enjoy." They were quite a team.

After graduation, Father Hugh enrolled at Holy Cross College, while my father entered Saint Mary's Seminary in Baltimore, Maryland. Ultimately, their roles were reversed, however; Father Hugh entered St. Mary's after graduating from Holy Cross, but my father had left the seminary by then. This turn of events led my father to sometimes joke that he couldn't leave the Church until he found his replacement. But, as the writings in this book attest, Father Hugh eliminated any notion of a replacement—he was *destined* to be a priest, and a remarkable one. He remained a great friend to our family as he distinguished himself as an outstanding and beloved parish priest. When my father died unexpectedly at the age of forty-four, Father Hugh's wisdom and comfort were immeasurable, as they continued to be for many years. He shared in our sorrows as well as our joys—he was the celebrant at my parents' wedding, as well as at my own to Cynthia, my wife. In fact, on the day of our wedding, Father Hugh shot a hole in one on the second hole—which I took as a good sign—a bit of Irish luck blessing us all that day.

Father Hugh's friendship and counsel remained a fortifying influence as I advanced in my own career as well. I looked forward to spending time with him while on the road as a newspaper syndicate salesman on the East Coast, staying at his parish while traveling throughout western Massachusetts. After a week of tolerating me at the rectory, I would host Father Hugh and his fellow priests for a nice night out with cocktails and a steak dinner (a treat that wasn't always welcomed by our accounting department when I submitted my expenses).

With his effervescent, dynamic personality, spending time with him and hearing his stories were highlights of my travels.

When Father Hugh learned of his Alzheimer's diagnosis, he accepted it with humility and grace, consistent with the manner he had conducted himself his whole life. Andrews McMeel Publishing, and myself in particular, are honored with this opportunity to share his insight with a wider audience. Readers will continue to be enriched by his wise words, as *Along the Way* continues his legacy.

Hugh T. Andrews
Chairman, Andrews McMeel Universal

Contributor Biographies

PETER A. DEPERGOLA II, PHD, was raised in Longmeadow, Massachusetts, and is a graduate of the College of Our Lady of the Elms. Following graduation from Elms College, Dr. DePergola attended Boston College, where he received a master's of theological studies degree in ethics. He subsequently received a doctoral degree in health care ethics from Duquesne University. A well-respected member of the Elms College faculty and executive director of the college's Saint Augustine Center for Ethics, Religion, and Culture, Dr. DePergola concurrently serves as chief ethics officer and senior director of clinical ethics at Baystate Health, whose flagship medical center is located in Springfield, Massachusetts. The recipient of numerous honors and awards for academic scholarship and health care leadership, his current research explores moral virtue and end-of-life decision making. At Elms College, Dr. DePergola is the Shaughness Family Chair for the Study of Humanities. His first book, *Forget Me Not: The Neuroethical Case Against Memory Manipulation* (Vernon Press, 2018), has been critically acclaimed as a landmark achievement in the field of neuroethics.

MARY B. JOHNSON, SNDDEN, PHD, was raised in Sacred Heart Parish, Springfield, Massachusetts, where she first met Father Hugh Crean. She attended Emmanuel College in Boston, where she majored in sociology and graduated in 1979. She entered religious life in 1981 and began her teaching career at Saint Gregory's High School in Dorchester, Massachusetts. Sister Mary holds a doctoral degree in sociology from the University of Massachusetts. She has served on the faculty of both Emmanuel College and Trinity Washington University. In 2020, Sister Mary delivered the inaugural Reverend Hugh Crean Distinguished Lecture at the College of Our Lady of the Elms. In 2021, Sister Mary was elected community leader of the Sisters of Notre Dame de Namur. She speaks nationally and internationally on issues related to Catholicism, religious life, and Catholic Social Teaching. In addition, Sister Mary has authored numerous articles and has coauthored several books, including *Migration for Mission: International Catholic Sisters in the United States* (Oxford University Press, 2019).

MICHAEL J. MCGRAVEY, PHD, a native of Buffalo, New York, completed his undergraduate work at Gannon University in Erie, Pennsylvania. He later received a master's of arts degree in theology and religious studies from Villanova University and a doctoral degree in systematic theology from Duquesne University. Between 2005 and 2009, Dr. McGravey taught at Saint Joseph's Preparatory School in Philadelphia. He subsequently served as a teaching assistant and instructor in the Department of Theology at Duquesne University. Dr. McGravey joined the faculty of the College of Our Lady of the Elms in 2020. In addition to his teaching responsibilities, Dr. McGravey directs the college's Institute for Theology and Pastoral Studies and is actively engaged in the work of several faculty committees. A frequent presenter at academic conferences, he blogs regularly on topics related to religion, theology, and excellence in undergraduate teaching. Dr. McGravey and his family are parishioners of Saint Mary's Parish in Longmeadow, Massachusetts.

JANE F. MORRISSEY, SSJ, PHD, is a native of Westfield, Massachusetts, and a lifelong friend of the Crean family. Sister Jane attended the College of Our Lady of the Elms in Chicopee, Massachusetts, where she majored in English and graduated in 1962. She entered the Sisters of St. Joseph of Springfield in 1963 and spent several years teaching at Cathedral High School in Springfield, Massachusetts. Upon completion of doctoral work at the University of Massachusetts, Sister Jane joined the faculty of Elms College, where she served for fourteen years in the Department of English. From 1990 to 1993, she directed her religious community's Office of Peace and Justice. In 1993, Sister Jane began work as a pastoral minister at Blessed Sacrament Parish in Springfield. Sister Jane was elected president of the Sisters of St. Joseph of Springfield in 1996 and served in that position until 2005. In 2006, Sister Jane became a cofounder of Homework House, which continues to serve the needs of children living in the inner city of Holyoke, Massachusetts.

DAVID J. O'BRIEN, PHD, grew up in Pittsfield, Massachusetts, where he was educated by the Sisters of St. Joseph of Springfield. He graduated from Notre Dame University in 1960 and holds a doctorate in history from the University of Rochester. A preeminent Catholic historian, Dr. O'Brien is professor emeritus of history at the College of the Holy Cross in Worcester, Massachusetts. He is past president of the American Catholic Historical Association and was one of the organizers of United States Catholic Bishops' 1976 Call to Action program. One of the first American historians to specialize in American Catholic history, Dr. O'Brien has written or edited numerous books. He has received countless accolades for his work, including the Theodore M. Hesburgh Award for Distinguished Contribution to Catholic Higher Education from the Association of Catholic Colleges and Universities. A former trustee and advisor to presidents of the College of Our Lady of the Elms, Dr. O'Brien delivered the annual Reverend Hugh Crean Distinguished Lecture at the College of Our Lady of the Elms in 2021.

Appendix

DIGITAL RESOURCES

Special thanks to Anthony Fonseca and Curtis Maloney for editing and digitizing these resources.

A. The lecture accessed through the link below is part of the Mary A. Dooley Lecture Series in Religious Studies, which continues to be sponsored by Elms College in Chicopee, Massachusetts. The lecture series began in 1986 with the topic of Vatican II: Twenty Years Later. Sister Mary A. Dooley was the sixth president of Elms College, serving in that capacity from 1979 to 1994. The lecture series topic for 1990–1991 was Envisioning the Church of Tomorrow, Today. This particular lecture, by Father Hugh Crean, who was at the time the Vicar of Priests for the Diocese of Springfield, Massachusetts, was held on February 25, 1991. https://archive.org/details/mary-a.-dooley-lecture-fr.-hugh-crean-1991

B. This lecture that follows is also part of the Mary A. Dooley Lecture Series in Religious Studies. The lecture series topic for 1995–1996 was Discovering the Sacred Within. This particular lecture, by Father Hugh Crean, who was at that time pastor of Holy Parish in Springfield, Massachusetts, was held on September 25, 1995. Its title was "Doubt and Faith, Shadow and Light: Signs of the Sacred Within." The original introduction to Father Crean was lost, so in 2021 Father Mark Stelzer recorded a new introduction, which can be heard on this recording. https://archive.org/details/mary-a.-dooley-lecture-fr.-hugh-crean-1995

C. On May 29, 1990, Father Hugh Crean was the celebrant of *The Chalice of Salvation,* a weekly televised Mass produced by the

Diocese of Springfield, Massachusetts. In attendance at the Mass were Sisters of Notre Dame de Namur, celebrating the 150th anniversary of their community's arrival in the United States. https://drive.google.com/file/d/1E8UHY6bnp0bIorDIVsU9uCAEaW_-dVmR/view

Inspiring Words from Father Hugh F. Crean

"Saints come in all sizes and shapes, nationalities, and personalities. It is not the size of the halo or piety that makes a saint. It is quality of life and goodness that make a saint."

"As we read through the pages of the New Testament, we can't help but notice that Jesus was constantly responding to all sorts of human needs. When people were sick, he healed them; when they were lonely, he included them; when they were ignorant, he taught them; when they sinned, he forgave them; when their hearts were broken, he comforted them; and when they were hungry, he fed them."

"Sisters, when you entered your community, you responded to the call of Abraham: "Come to the place to which I will show you." (Genesis 12:1) Like Abraham, you followed that call. My sincere prayer is that you continue to hear and follow that call in these golden and diamond years of ministry."

"A school is a house of formation, a tradition maker, a value center, a memory bank. A Catholic school is a sanctuary, a home, a family. It is a place where not only math and science and literature are taught, but also values and virtues. A Catholic school is about God and Jesus Christ. It is about the Gospel and faith. A Catholic school is about human rights and values."

"My dear people, we have such eloquent reasons for faith and hope. Regardless of any darkness caused by any financial, physical, or emotional problems which surround us, the light of Christ shines forth and overcomes all darkness."

"What can we say to our senior priests? Each of you has already invested so much of your life. You have been an amazing grace to so many people in your years of ministry. We ask you today to encourage us as we become involved in the issues of our day, just as you passionately cared for the causes of your youth and middle years. You still have a ministry to share. Like Simeon and Anna, you optimistically proclaim the beginning of a new day."

Andrews McMeel Publishing
a division of Andrews McMeel Universal
1130 Walnut Street, Kansas City, Missouri 64106

www.andrewsmcmeel.com

22 23 24 25 26 VEP 10 9 8 7 6 5 4 3 2 1

ISBN: 978-1-5248-7473-5

Library of Congress Control Number: 2022935905

Editor: Jean Z. Lucas
Art Director/Designer: Abby Gust
Production Editor: Elizabeth A. Garcia
Production Manager: Shona Burns